IAI
The Art of Drawing The Sword

IAI-JITSU

center of the circle
by DARRELL CRAIG

CHARLES E. TUTTLE COMPANY
Rutland, Vermont & Tokyo, Japan

Published by the Charles E. Tuttle Company, Inc.
of Rutland, Vermont & Tokyo, Japan
with editorial offices at
153 Milk Street, Boston, MA 02109

Library of Congress Catalog Card Number 83-193519
ISBN 0-8048-7023-3

First edition published in 1981 by Lotus Press Ltd.,
Chofu PO Box 15, Chofu-shi, Tokyo 182-91, Japan

First Tuttle edition - 1988
00 99 98 97 96   7 9 10 8

Cover design by Jill Haber

PRINTED IN THE UNITED STATES

This book is dedicated in memory of
Sensei Mori Torao, Master 8th-dan
Hanshi.

The author Darrell Craig studied Iai-Do under the scrtinizing eyes of Sensei Harutane Chiba of the Hokushin Style of Kendo in Osaka Japan.

Mr. Craig and Master Shogo Kuniba

A 1974 photograph of Master Ichiro Hata (center), Sensei Jutaro Yajima at a Kendo clinic in Houston, Texas. Mr. Craig is back row, far right.

Master Kuniba in kata of Mu-Gai-Ryu

Contents

Acknowledgments

Horibe Yahyoe Kanemaru   (Ronin of AKO)

BEGINNER'S MIND: "*In the beginner's mind there are many possibilities, but in the expert's there are few.*"

The characters for "beginner's" mind, brushed by Darrell Craig.

Zen Mind, Beginner's Mind by Shunryu Suzuki

If not looking for the end,
do you not always find the beginning?

Acknowledgments

I wish to express my sincere appreciation to my wife for her patience and for her typing. Also to:

Mrs. Violet Clark, for her time.

Mr. Terry Burge, for editing.

Mrs. Mary Schultz and Mr. Mark Hunter, for illustrations.

Mr. Joseph L. Rachel, for photography.

Without their help, this book would only be half-finished.

Introduction

Spiritual Guidance Between Buddhist Priest, Sōbōjō, and a Samurai Warrior, Usaiwakamaru.

To me, Iai-do is really unexplainable in all of its facets and depth, and I found myself starting and stopping this book more times than I care to remember. I always felt that there was some better way to explain something or that there were so many people with much more experience than I who could explain it more thoroughly. But what really encouraged me to write this book was this experience: One day I was out driving and saw a young man in a field cutting weeds with a Japanese sword, so I stopped the car and went over to ask if I might see the tool that he was using. At first glance I could see that the tip was broken off and that the edge had many chips in it. Nevertheless I took the handle off and was amazed to find that it was a very old blade. Now when I say old, I mean one or two hundred years old and not old as the Japanese think of a sword. I asked him where he found the sword, to which he replied, "Oh, my Dad got it in the war someplace." How many times have I heard that before? Then and there I knew that I had to finish this book.

I feel that every man on this earth has something to contribute to the subject which he loves, and I can say without any remorse that I have a love affair with the Japanese sword.

One day I was practicing the draws in Iai-do. I was doing them to the best of my ability, but I always felt that something was missing. I asked my Master what was wrong. He told me "Ken wa hito nari" or, "The sword is a person." I will use many such quotations in this book for several reasons. First, the authors of such quotations say what I feel so much better than I could and second when you are dealing with Iai-do and truly want to understand it, you must look to Zen.

Iai-do and Kendo go hand in hand. It would be easy to learn Kendo or the way of the sword without knowing Iai-do, but to learn Iai-do without knowing Kendo would be like dressing up in a tuxedo and going nowhere. Kendo and Iai-do can best be described by saying that Kendo is the art when the sword is out of the scabbard, while Iai-do consists of four movements: (1) Nukitsuke, or draw, (2) the Kiritsuke, or cutting movement, (3) the Chiburi, or removing the blood from the sword, and (4) the Noto, or return of the sword to its saya or scabbard. Both arts have their own fields and purposes. Kendo goes back to Kenjutsu (about A. D. 939) in Japanese history, while Iai-do takes the place of Iai-jutsu which some historians say Hojo Jinsuke developed in the seventeenth century. Nevertheless, after its development, there were some 400 different ryu's officially catalogued. The two we are concerned with here are the Iai-do of the Japanese Kendo Federation and Mu-Gai-Ryu. In 1959 or 1960, the Japanese Kendo Federation selected seven basic techniques from several different Ryu (styles) and grouped the seven forms to make up this Ryu. With the limitations of the Japanese Kendo Federation's Iai-do with just its seven kata or forms, I feel the reader may want to go further into Iai, so I have added Mu-Gai-Ryu. It is a very old Ryu and almost extinct in Japan today. You have to remember that some techniques and their applications were so secret that they were only passed on by word of mouth and were lost with the lapse of time.

I think it would be good to note at this time that only the Samurai were allowed to learn either Iai-do or Ken Arts. Ah, the Ṣamurai! It is easy to say the word Samurai but to explain the Samurai and his code of chivalry is indeed a book and a lifetime study in itself. It is my opinion that no other knight or warrior in this period of history had as much prestige or a harder code of honor to live by than these men of Japan. From about the sixteenth century until the prohibition of the wearing of swords in 1867, the Samurai wore two swords called Daishō (Lit., large and small). The small sword was worn across the belly with the edge turned up and pushed through the warrior's obi or belt. This sword went with him at all times, while the katana or long sword was worn to the left side with the cutting edge up and pushed through the belt. The katana had to be removed when entering a house or anytime he was summoned to an official's quarters. In the first place, the long sword got in the way indoors , where the ceilings were quite low. While a Samurai could do Iai-jutsu with the wakizashi (short sword) or long sword, most all Iai did evolve around the latter. In this period of time the rigorous training methods of Iai were one hundred and twenty draws with the katana and one thousand cuts per day. Today, in the twentieth century, twenty-five draws and about fifty cuts constitute a good workout.

Many men have said to me how wonderful it would have been to be a Samurai in that time in Japanese history. To this, I usually reply, "You mean that you could lay down your life at a moment's notice without asking why?"

Needless to say, it makes no sense to argue for the preservation of any martial art or its traditions. I believe in judging the merit of Kendo and Iai-do from an open standpoint, on its worth to the individual and the society. You can put this in one simple question: will the understanding of the art benefit me more than just copying a set of mechanical motions? If the answer is yes, then the decision that one must make is self-evident. Although some people have called Iai-do a religion, I find this hard to accept. However, I must also point out that though I do not consider it a religion, it is so interwoven with certain religious beliefs that they are inseparable. Iai-do is a result of generations of development in Japan, and while the West uses it for self-expression, the Japanese used it for mind improvement. Thus, while the outward body movements may be the same, the difference in attitudes is great. Mere technical knowledge is not enough to master Iai-do. You must go deeply into the inner spirit of the art. Training in Iai-do can only be successful when you have absorbed the mental as well as the physical techniques so that they are so much a part of you that using them is purely intuitive and unconscious. Your attitude should be one of alertness mixed with calmness and fearlessness. Therefore, it would be impossible to realize the outcome of the draw in a Kata, (form of practice). If you were to ask a Japanese Master of Ken (swords) to explain Iai-do, he would probably look at you for a minute trying to decide whether you really wanted to know or were just curious. No matter what he decided, he would most likely tell you it is very hard to explain in English or that there are many words in the English language that do not have quite the same meanings as their presumed Japanese equivalents. At that time he would change the subject very carefully to something else and before you knew what had happened, you might have forgotten that you had asked the question in the first place.

One of the words he was looking for in English is spirit, but here again I must tell you that the English word spirit does not quite mean the same as the Japanese word he would have chosen, which is mushin. Mushin means no-mind-ness or Munen, no-thoughtness. When practicing Iai-do, you must create a consciousness free from all thoughts or reflections or distractions of any kind. The best way to explain this is to tell you that the sword must become as much a part of you as your leg is. When you do something, it just moves. When picking up a sword, most people handle it as an extension of the arm, as if it were a very long hand or finger. When you can do Iai-do as if you were eating, with the elbow bending and the mouth opening without stopping for your brain to tell you each individual motion needed to move a spoon to your mouth, then it is natural. Your reactions in Iai-do must be as natural as eating: "You are said to have mastered the art when the technique works through your body and limbs as if independent of your conscious mind."[1]

[1]D. T. Suzuki, *Zen and Japanese Culture* (Princeton, N. J.: Princeton University Press, 1971). pp. 74

CHAPTER ONE

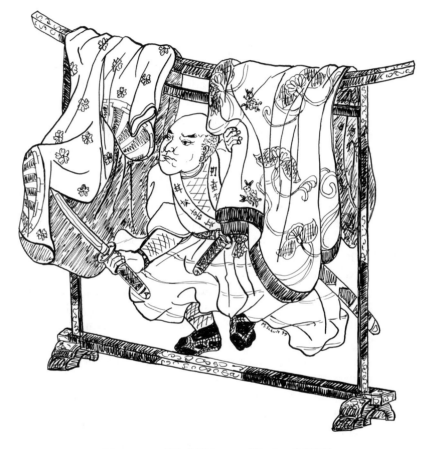

Muramatsu Kihei Hidenao   (Ronin of AKO)

Examining and Sword Servicing

"And when the Swordsmith handed it to me:
> All who beheld it said a long and whispered "Ahhh" at
> the strip of silver steel made with love and skill for the
> single purpose of opening live human flesh.[2]"

I knew it was mine and when I learned all there was to know about
it, it became me, and I became it. It gave me the soul I was
searching for, and I gave it the heart to come alive. Together we
saved many lives.

> For the Japanese the sword is more than just a weapon. It
> has mysterious powers like the cross to the Christians. It
> is felt that the sword receives its "soul" from the swor-
> dsmith during the forging and tempering process. It is for
> this reason that swordsmiths were treated with respect
> equal to, if not greater than, that given a priest.[4]

The entire manufacturing process was a ritual that began with the
swordsmith fasting and making prayers to the God of his forge and
ended with the quenching of the sword in a manner learned
through many years of work and study.

The swordsmith, through the strength and charity of his efforts,
is felt to take part of his soul, blend it with energy from the Gods
and this becomes the soul of the sword. Each sword is felt to reflect
the true "Self" of its maker.

> As something of divinity enters into the making of the
> sword, its owner and user ought also to respond to the
> inspiration. He ought to be a spiritual man, not an agent
> of brutality.[3]

The nomenclature of a sword is simple in some aspects and
complex in others. I am by no means an expert in the science of

---

[2]W. D. Jennings, *The Ronin* (Rutland, VT.: Charles E. Tuttle Co., 1968), p. 129
[3]D. T. Suzuki, *Zen and Japanese Culture* (Princeton, N.J.: Princeton University Press, 1971), p. 93
[4]Rodger Fitlock, 'Japanese Cross," *Black Belt Magazine*, 7–5 (May 1969) 49

swords. This I leave to men in that field. My contribution is to let the people who have a Japanese sword know a little something about it, and, if they are interested, to learn an art with it. As you can see by the drawings, swords have many different tangs or ends that go under the wooden handle. This part of the blade is where the date and signature are found. One must remember just because the Tang does not have a signature or a date, does not mean that it is not valuable. You could have a very old date and maker's name on the Tang and it may be worthless. On the other hand, an unsigned Tang could be worth a small fortune. Please let me interject this small note: just because you have a Japanese sword, do not let me make you think that you necessarily have an heirloom. I must also point out that there are a lot of Japanese swords just lying around in garages or attics from World War II that are waiting to be found.

Let me tell you about a friend of mine that we will call Mr. Goodnow. As he and I became better acquainted he started taking up the Martial Arts from me and he was telling a friend of his about me, Iai-do, swords, and one thing and another. This friend one day went to his grandfather's farm out in the country and there in the barn in the corner were two Japanese swords. Now not knowing anything about them, but remembering what Mr. Goodnow had said, he brought them back to town for me to examine. The thing I would like to point out here is that no one had touched those swords since 1945. They were out there all that time, by some miracle in a dry place, leaning up against a post with a rat's nest at the bottom. When I pulled the blades out of the scabbard, we were all shocked at their mirror-like finish. Not one piece of rust anyplace. Nervously, I pulled off the handles. One proved to be worth about eight hundred dollars and the other worth a couple of hundred dollars. You never know exactly what you have until you examine it thoroughly and get an expert's opinion.

Never, and I repeat never, put your fingers on the blade. The blade is made up of five parts, the shinogi (back side one half the way down from the handle), the Hamon (temper pattern along the cutting edge), the Mune (back side about eight inches back from the

4

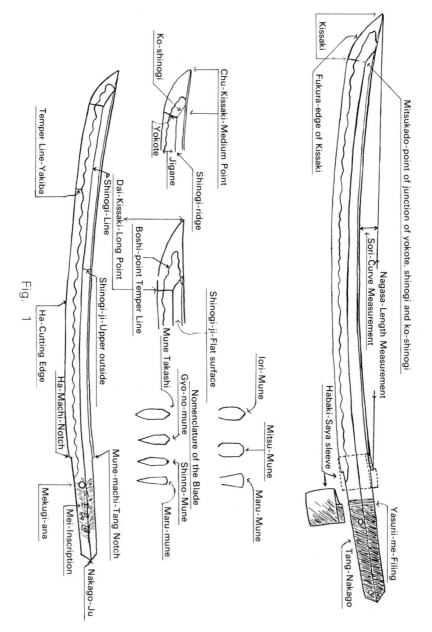

Fig. 1

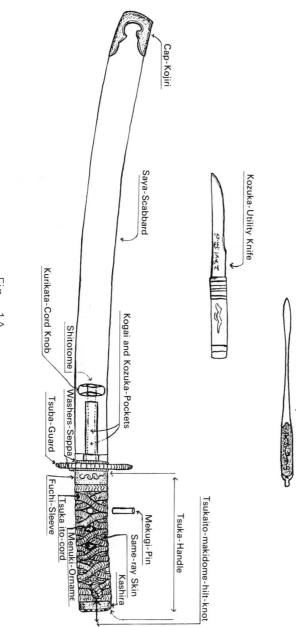

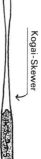

Fig. 1A

Cap-Kojiri

Saya-Scabbard

Kozuka-Utility Knife

Kogai-Skewer

Kurikata-Cord Knob

Shitotome

Kogai and Kozuka-Pockets

Washers-Seppa

Tsuba-Guard

Tsukaito-makidome-hilt-knot

Tsuka-Handle

Mekugi-Pin

Same-ray Skin

Kashira

Tsuka ito-cord

Menuki-Orname

Fuchi-Sleeve

6

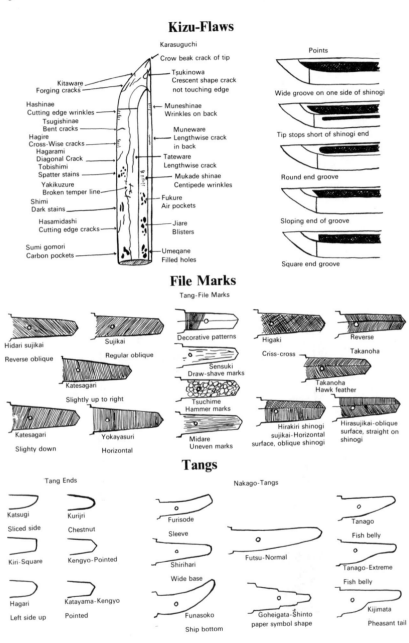

Kizu-Flaws

Karasuguchi
Crow beak crack of tip

Tsukinowa
Crescent shape crack
not touching edge

Kitaware
Forging cracks

Hashinae
Cutting edge wrinkles
Tsugishinae
Bent cracks
Hagire
Cross-Wise cracks
Hagarami
Diagonal Crack
Tobishimi
Spatter stains
Yakikuzure
Broken temper line
Shimi
Dark stains

Hasamidashi
Cutting edge cracks

Sumi gomori
Carbon pockets

Muneshinae
Wrinkles on back

Muneware
Lengthwise crack
in back

Tateware
Lengthwise crack

Mukade shinae
Centipede wrinkles

Fukure
Air pockets

Jiare
Blisters

Umeqane
Filled holes

Points

Wide groove on one side of shinogi

Tip stops short of shinogi end

Round end groove

Sloping end of groove

Square end groove

File Marks

Tang-File Marks

Hidari sujikai
Reverse oblique

Sujikai
Regular oblique

Katesagari

Slightly up to right

Katesagari
Slighty down

Yokayasuri
Horizontal

Decorative patterns

Sensuki
Draw-shave marks

Tsuchime
Hammer marks

Midare
Uneven marks

Higaki
Criss-cross

Takanoha
Hawk feather

Hirakiri shinogi
sujikai-Horizontal
surface, oblique shinogi

Reverse
Takanoha

Hirasujikai-oblique
surface, straight on
shinogi

Tangs

Tang Ends

Katsugi
Sliced side

Kurijri
Chestnut

Kiri-Square

Kengyo-Pointed

Hagari
Left side up

Katayama-Kengyo
Pointed

Nakago-Tangs

Furisode
Sleeve

Shirihari
Wide base

Funasoko
Ship bottom

Futsu-Normal

Goheigata-Shinto
paper symbol shape

Tanago
Fish belly

Tanago-Extreme
Fish belly

Kijimata
Pheasant tail

Fig. 2

Yakiba—Temper Lines

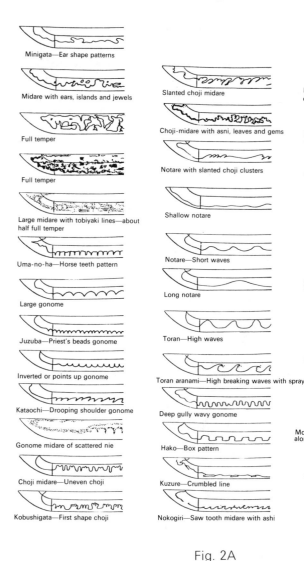

Minigata—Ear shape patterns

Midare with ears, islands and jewels

Full temper

Full temper

Large midare with tobiyaki lines—about half full temper

Uma-no-ha—Horse teeth pattern

Large gonome

Juzuba—Priest's beads gonome

Inverted or points up gonome

Kataochi—Drooping shoulder gonome

Gonome midare of scattered nie

Choji midare—Uneven choji

Kobushigata—First shape choji

Slanted choji midare

Choji-midare with asni, leaves and gems

Notare with slanted choji clusters

Shallow notare

Notare—Short waves

Long notare

Toran—High waves

Toran aranami—High breaking waves with spray

Deep gully wavy gonome

Hako—Box pattern

Kuzure—Crumbled line

Nokogiri—Saw tooth midare with ashi

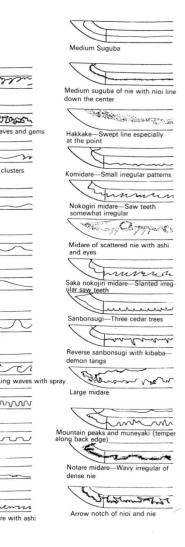

Medium Suguba

Medium suguba of nie with nioi line down the center

Hakkake—Swept line especially at the point

Komidare—Small irregular patterns

Nokogiri midare—Saw teeth somewhat irregular

Midare of scattered nie with ashi and eyes

Saka nokojiri midare—Slanted irregular saw teeth

Sanbonsugi—Three cedar trees

Reverse sanbonsugi with kibaba—demon tangs

Large midare

Mountain peaks and muneyaki (temper along back edge)

Notare midare—Wavy irregular of dense nie

Arrow notch of nioi and nie

Fig. 2A

end), the Monouchi (first eight inches of the cutting edge), and the Kissaki (tip). (See Figure #1.) There are two reasons for not touching the blade. First and most important, the ha or cutting edge being of surgical sharpness will cut you, and secondly, moisture and acids in one's hands will begin to make it rust in a matter of minutes. Take a clean piece of soft paper or cloth and hold the back side while you are looking at it. Look for Kizu, or flaws. (See Figure #2.) Next, look at the Hamon, this can be very exciting since there are so many different patterns, and the work-

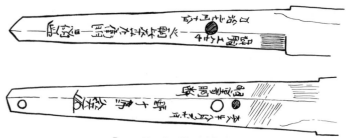

Tangs with mei and Testing Certification

Tsuba with mei

Fig. 2B

manship is so beautiful. The Kissaki is the last thing you should examine. If you hold the sword in the light, it will bring out the beauty even more. Never attempt to sharpen or polish the blade. The Japanese use a series of fine stones to sharpen and bring out the grain of the steel which could be forever lost by inexperienced buffing. If there are small rust spots, they can be removed by using some coarse paper (not sand paper). Something else that I have found helpful to bring out the luster of the blade is silver polish.

There are many types of Japanese swords and not all are the long katanas which we usually think about. For instance, we have the Tachi (slung sword). Dai katana (horse sword), standard Samurai katana, Wakizashi (short sword). Tanto (dagger), Aikuchi (dagger

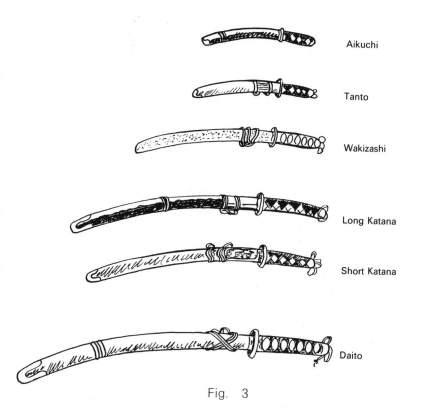

Aikuchi

Tanto

Wakizashi

Long Katana

Short Katana

Daito

Fig. 3

without tsuba), and the Heyazashi (a small tanto carried in the clothing). All of these blades had a specific purpose and should be handled with the same care as the katana. See Figure #3.

If you are looking for a Samurai sword to buy or have one to sell, let me give you a word of warning. You should be careful. It is always better to buy from a known collector rather than from a dealer. Here again, it depends on the quality of blade that you wish to buy or to sell. I think that it is safe to say that the worth of the blade is highly subjective and may be only determined by the person who is buying or selling it. But remember, a collector usually collects quality and a dealer buys and sells only for a living. Many times dealers make a very good living off of the unknowing customers.

I have noticed in the past few years that at gun shows, the Samurai swords for sale have gone down in quality and up in price. This is contributed to by two factors: First, many swords are disappearing and secondly, blades are being sold back and forth from dealer to dealer.

I know that in this part of the country, since the Martial Arts boom, everyone who has taken up a Martial Art has had to own a Samurai sword. This has boosted the price of a twenty dollar sword to about one hundred dollars. The person who knows a little about the swords would not want that kind of a blade. However, some enthusiasts simply have to possess one, no matter what the quality. For instance, a dealer whom I know told me last year that he would buy all the "junk" blades that I could get my hands on. He said, "These kids are buying up things we could not have given away last year at more than a hundred bucks each and we are making a killing"

Let us look at what makes a little better than average katana. First, it should be around 31 3/4 inches in length (from the hamachi or edge notch to the kissaki or point). (See Figure #1.) Next, look under the handle at the tang. Slide back the habaki or scabbard sleeve and look for a small cherry blossom stamp. If it is there, then you know at once that it is a new blade and made sometime during the Showa Era (1926 to present). I once heard a dealer tell a prospective customer to look at all the matching numbers on the blade and on the hardware. "That makes this a collectors' item." The customer bought the sword for three hundred dollars. Last year the dealer would have been lucky to get fifteen dollars for it. Remember that doing business at a large gun show is like buying a used car from Crazy Harry's Used Car Lot. Crazy Harry is crazy like a fox.

If you are only going to invest a minimum amount, say seventy-five or one hundred dollars, do not expect to get much for your money. Try to get a blade without too many pits or chips. If possible, get a sword with a wooden saya, no matter what shape it is in, you can always repair it or have it repaired for a minimal cost. The blade is what you are most concerned with. If it is clean, not too heavy, and most importantly—if you can afford it—buy it. If you buy too expensive a sword to begin with, you might damage it while you are beginning to learn Iai-do. If you are going to invest several hundred dollars in a sword, I suggest that you either find someone who knows about swords or that you try to read as much as possible about them. There are several good books on Japanese swords in English. The library has many of these books or you can buy them. Remember that fifteen to thirty dollars invested in books on the subject is much better than three hundred dollars lost by not being sure what you have.

No matter what kind of a katana you buy, take care of it. It is one of a kind and most important, it is yours. If you can learn Iai-do with it, it will become you, with both your shortcomings and imagination. You would not let someone open your head and touch your brain, so do not let anyone pull your sword from its saya and touch the skin. The swords of Japan have been said to be "the living souls of the Samurai." They were "the pride of Warriors and the theme of Pacts"[4]

The Samurai had just two things that were his and his alone. No man could take them from him. First was his honor and next it was his swords. His sword was regarded as the truest emblem of his

[4]B.W. Robinson, *The Arts of the Japanese Sword* (C. E. Tuttle, Co. Inc., Rutland, Vermont: 1971), p. 15

virtue, valor, and strength. Mottos such as:

> There is nothing between heaven and earth that man need fear who carries at his side this magnificent blade.[5]

To exemplify this idea. The Samurai believed that:

> All weapons meant to kill are inconspicuous and never must be used except on occasions of extreme urgency. If any at all is to be used, however, let it be known that it is for the purpose of punishing evil and not for depriving one of life.[6]

I feel that it is very important to note at this time (see Figure #4) the five elements of the universe; earth, metal, fire, water, and wood. All take their part in making the Japanese sword.

[5]Donn F. Draeger, *Asian Fighting Arts* (Berkley Publishing Corp.: N.Y, N.Y.) p. 101

[6]D. T. Suzuki, *Zen and the Japanese Culture* (Princeton, N.J.: Princeton University Press, 1971)

Fig. 4

Fig. 4

Formal Examining of the Katana

The strictest of rules were observed by the Samurai in ancient times for examining the katana. Remember if you are a beginner in handling the sword, be extremely careful. First, because of the sharpness, and second, because if you drop the blade, you might damage or destroy its value as an object of great art.

First, you should purchase a cleaning kit which consists of oil,

Fig. 5

cleaning powder, and a brass tapper. Find a quiet place where you will not be disturbed. Take your katana out of its bag. Start by showing it the respect due a strange person being introduced to you for the first time. You would shake hands in this country. But in Japan they would bow, so you should now bow to the blade. (See Figures # 5 and 5A.)

Now holding the sword with your left hand, ha up, about half way down the saya, look at the kodogu or furniture. The furniture consists of all the metal ornaments and fittings on the sword except the blade itself. It is interesting to note that sometimes the kodogu are more valuable than the katana. Some pieces are made of gold and silver. Even the tsuba at times are signed and may be very valuable. Still holding the katana with your left hand and with the

Fig. 5A

cutting edge up, start to pull the blade from the saya. (See Figure #6.)

This should be done slowly. It is important to pull the saya from the katana and not the katana from the saya. Pull the blade out until you reach the kissaki. When you reach the kissaki, stop and examine it carefully. It is the most important part of the blade. When you have taken the sword all the way out of the saya, you may proceed to examine the blade. Laying down the saya, you may hold the sword in either hand. (See Figure #7.) Remember that it is not proper to examine the blade while you are taking it from the saya.

Fig. 6

The best way to examine the blade now that it is out of the saya is to take a piece of soft clean cloth in one hand and rest the shinogi on it. (See Figure #8.) While you are examining the blade, be sure not to turn the ha or cutting edge toward anyone but yourself: this is most important.

After examining the blade for new rust marks, take the small

Fig. 7

brass taper and remove the pin from the tsuba or handle. Taking the tsuba toward the bottom, in your right hand let the blade slant 35°. Next, with the cutting edge up, hit your own right wrist with your left fist until the blade pops up. (See Figure #9.)

When the blade is loose from the handle, put the blade back in the saya. Now that the blade is safely put away, remove the tsuba from the tang or nakago. At this time you should remove all the hardware from the tang. Sometimes the habaki is very hard to remove, but if you work with it by using the brass taper, it will come off easily. After examining the nakago, remove the blade again from the saya, using your right hand and the soft cloth in your left. The blade is now ready for cleaning. (See Figure #10.) Note that cleaning can be done with or without the handle in place.

Fig. 8

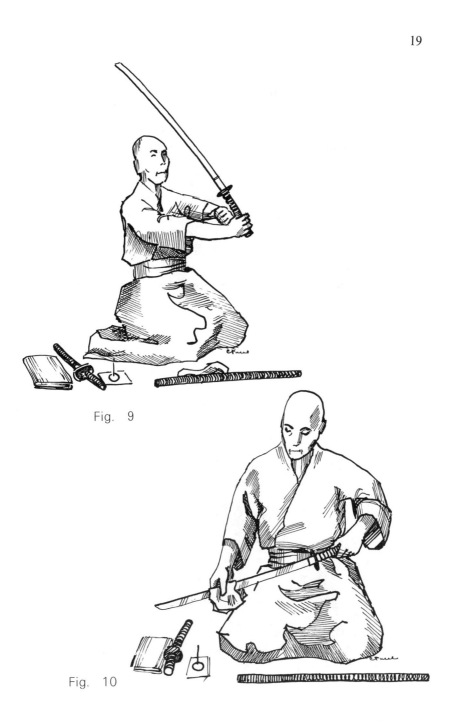

Fig. 9

Fig. 10

Cleaning of the Katana

The first thing in cleaning the blade is to remove any oil that is now on it. After doing this, take the small round red ball that is in your cleaning kit (it has powdered limestone in it, called uchiko) and powder the entire blade. (See Figure #11.)

After you have powdered the blade, take your cloth and give the blade forty to forty-five strokes on each side, always going up the blade from the back side so as not to cut yourself. The Samurai cleaned their swords everyday with forty to forty-five strokes. Always be very careful with the cleaning action; remember that if you get careless, the sword has a mind of its own and will remind you very painfully of your mistakes. After you have finished, wipe

Fig. 11

the blade clean with your cloth and go over the blade with the oil provided in your kit. There are several oils which you may use, such as mineral or vegetable, but the Japanese sword oil is the best, being made from cloves. After the blade has been serviced, replace all hardware and the handle, being careful not to touch the skin of the blade. After you have replaced the sword in the saya, cutting edge up, so that you do not drag the edge on the saya, replace it in your sword bag. This formal cleaning is only necessary about three or four times each year. But remember, when learning Iai-do, you must clean the blade each and every time your lesson is finished. The cleaning after lessons consists only of wiping the blade down with a clean cloth; you need not use the powdered limestone. The powdered limestone has a cutting action like sandpaper and if used

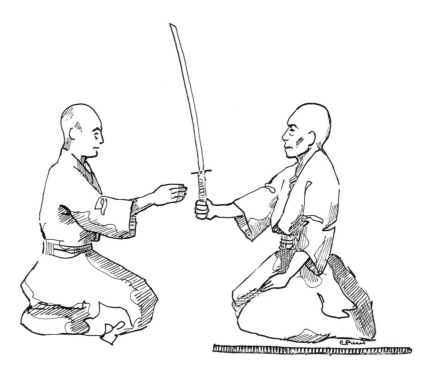

Fig. 12

excessively, it will eventually take the yakiba off. After you have wiped the blade, put a thin coat of oil on it and return the blade to the saya. Take your time, get to know your Katana; it is probably a lot older than you.

One of the last things I would like to mention is how to show someone your sword. (See Figure #12.) If someone asks to see your katana and you wish him to look at it, always take the bottom part of the handle in your right hand, leaving plenty of room for the other person's hand. Place the cutting edge toward yourself and make sure that they have a firm grip on the handle before letting go.

CHAPTER TWO

Kayano Wasuke Tsunenari   (Ronin of AKO)

Uniform Procedure

Hakama

The Iai-do-gi consists of two pieces: the top jacket which can be white or dark blue and the hakama. The white and black stitched top is usually worn by beginners. The hakama most commonly worn in practice is dark blue or black. Never mix your top and bottoms, like white top with a black bottom or black top with a white bottom. Of course, if you are a beginner, then the white top with the black stitching and the dark hakama is quite proper.

The hakama allows complete movement and its big bell-bottoms permit good air circulation when you are practicing Iai-do.

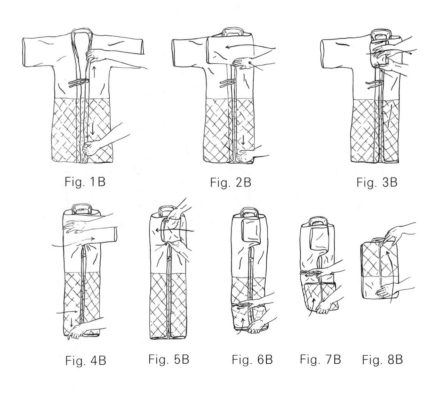

Fig. 1B   Fig. 2B   Fig. 3B

Fig. 4B   Fig. 5B   Fig. 6B   Fig. 7B   Fig. 8B

Figures #*1B* through #*8B* show you how to fold your top after practice. Never crumple-up your uniform after practice, remember the uniform is yours. Treat it with respect.

Putting on the hakama (Figure #*1C*). As you step into the hakama, put the koshi-ita or stiffener to the back.

Now, pull the front up, take hold of the cords, wrap them behind you, and, changing hands, bring the cords to the front again. (See Figure #*2C*.)

Now, crossing the cords in front about three inches down from the top waist band. (see Figure #*3C*.)

Pull the cords to the rear and tie them in a bow. Make sure that your top is pulled down tight so that there is not a bulge in the back. (See Figure #*4C*.)

Now pick up the back of the hakama with both hands. Place the koshi-ita over the bow and bring the cords to the front. (See Figure #*5C*.)

Figures #*3C & 6C* shows that all cords, front and back, are in line crossing to the front. Tie a small knot in the center where the cords cross.

Fig. 1C

Fig. 2C

Fig. 3C

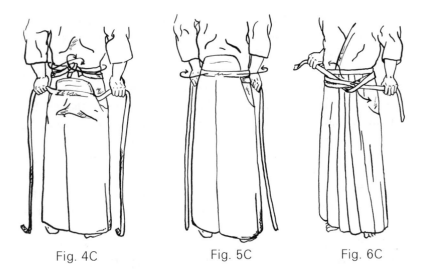

Fig. 4C   Fig. 5C   Fig. 6C

After this take one end and fold it back and forth across the knot (see Figure #7C), making all ends even.

When this is finished, take the other end and circle around the bow until there is nothing left. (See Figure #8C.)

When you finish, it should look like Figure #9C, with no ends showing.

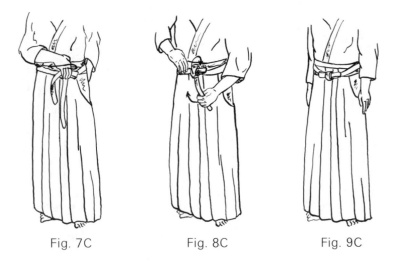

Fig. 7C   Fig. 8C   Fig. 9C

Sageo

Sageo is the Japanese word used for the cord on the saya or scabbard. It has many uses, but the most important one to the Samurai or Bushi was for tying the sleeves of his kimono up out of the way to prepare for action.

I should point out that there are as many Ryu (or schools) for the sageo as there are for Iai-do. It would be safe to say each style of Iai-do usually has its own Sageo method. Here we are dealing with the Mu-Gai-Ryu method.

Figure #13 illustrates making your formal bow and sitting in place (Seiza).

With the katana on your left side, the cutting edge away from you and the tsuba even with your left knee, take the sageo out of the kurigata. Note that this action may also be done after the katana is in the obi (or belt). Then, taking the sageo in your left hand, place one end in your mouth. (See Figure #14.)

Fig. 13   Fig. 14

Now, extending the right hand about three-fourths of the way out, use the left hand and place the sageo behind the right arm and behind the neck. Pull the sleeve up snug. (See Figure #15.)

Now using the right hand, take the sageo behind the left shoulder, catching the left sleeve, and bring it in front of the left arm and behind the neck, taking hold of the sageo with the right hand. (See Figure #16.)

Figure #17 shows a bow tied in the sageo over the right shoulder.

Figure #18 shows that the bow has been removed from sight by

Fig.　15

Fig.　16

Fig.　17

Fig.　18

pulling on the sageo with the right hand using the sageo under the left arm.

Remember that the beginning of practice is as important as the end. The tying of the sageo by a sixteenth-century Samurai preparing for battle was indeed a sight to behold. The tying of the sageo could be done in about three seconds and with one hand. If the opposing Samurai could see that his opponent had mastered the sageo with the speed of lightning, but yet the stillness of a forest just before a storm, he might think twice before doing battle.

CHAPTER THREE

Chikamatsu Kanroku Yukishige   (Ronin of AKO)

Iaido Dojo

Proper Sword Procedure
Iaido Dojo

You should always be aware of the tradition of the performance of Iai before a Shinto altar or before friends. Most importantly, never make a circus out of Iai. People will respect you and the art more—even if they themselves do not understand it—if you maintain the etiquette that the art deserves.

Fig. 19

TEITO SHISEI:

Teito Shisei is the formal standing position before you enter the dojo or place in which you are about to practice. (See Figure #19.)

The katana or long sword is in the left hand with the cutting edge turned up. Your thumb should always be on the tsuba or sword guard at all times when you are moving the katana from one place to another or when you are carrying the sword. With the katana in the left hand, turn the end of the handle to the right one-half way between your navel and your right side with the end of the saya or scabbard pointing down about thirty to thirty-five degrees. The thumb on the left hand should slightly touch the waist or upper hipbone, depending on one's build. The left elbow is bent about twenty degrees and is relaxed. (Note that you should always remain relaxed—in *every* move).

Carrying the Katana

Always remember that the katana is a very dangerous weapon and that the Japanese have a great respect for it, as you will also if you know what you are doing when you carry one.

Note that you should never take the katana out of the saya or scabbard in jest or act as if you are about to draw it against someone. You would not take a real gun out and point it at another, unless you intended to do him harm: the Japanese feel the same way about the sword.

If you are in the dojo, the foot closest to the shrine or flag is the "upper foot." Go to the place in which you are going to practice with the shrine or flag on your left side. This is your front during the exercise. To change your direction, turn in the direction of your "upper foot". This "upper foot" is called Kami-no-ashi.

The Formal Bow or Kamiza

Holding the katana in your left hand, handle to the front, blade slanting down about thirty five degrees, stand erect, facing the shrine or flag. (See Figure #19.) Now reach across your body and take the katana below the saya or sword guard. (See Figure #*20*.)

Next bring the katana to the right side of the body with the handle to the rear with the cutting edge pointing down and the kojiri pointing down thirty-five degrees. You must remember to stay completely relaxed. (See Figure #*21*.)

Now bow from the waist toward the shrine, flag, or dojo. Try to keep your head in line with your back. (See Figure #*22*.)

Fig. 20

After the bow, take your left hand and grasp the saya below the tsuba and replace the katana on the left side of the body. (See Figure #23.)

Place your thumb on the tsuba. During outdoor practice, you may hold the katana horizontally above your head and bow.

Fig. 21

Fig. 22

Fig. 23

Sitting in Place: Seiza

Holding the katana in your left hand, thumb on the tsuba, bend your knees about forty degrees. Then reach down with your right hand and spread the hakama or skirt. This can be done quietly by pushing the loose material left to right behind the knees. Now kneel in place, first with the left knee and then the right. Try and keep your back as straight as possible. You should fix your eyes at a point about three feet in front of you on the floor. (See Figure #24.)

As you sit, bring both big toes together; and your feet should make a "v". (See Figure #25.)

Fig. 24

The knees should be about six to seven inches apart. Place your right hand on your right thigh and the katana on the left thigh. (See Figure #26.)

Now lay the katana to the left side of your left thigh, with the sword guard in line with your knee. The cutting edge must be turned toward your own body, about six inches away from your thigh. (See Figure #27.)

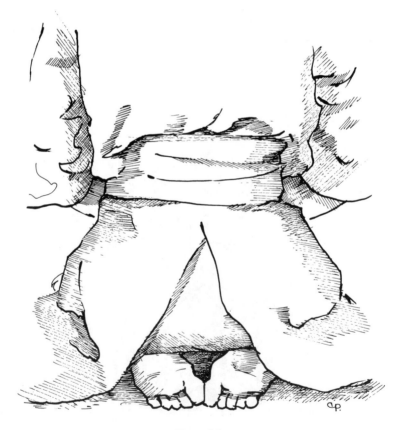

Fig. 25

This is one of the most important parts of Iai-do. You must sit erect, straightening the neck and the chest. Close your eyes and place both hands on your thighs. You must be completely relaxed at this point:

> Try to clear your mind of all things. This is called Mushin.
> Remember "The moon has no intent to cast its shadow
> anywhere, nor does the pond design to lodge the moon."[1]

After one or two minutes, open your eyes half way and focus them about six-feet in front of you on the floor, forming a triangle with the fingers and touching the thumbs. (See Figure #28.)

Your upper body should be leaning forward about forty-five degrees. As you formally bow, both elbows touch the knees and the floor. Hold the bow for about a slow five count, then rise slowly

[1]Ibid pp 116

Fig. 26

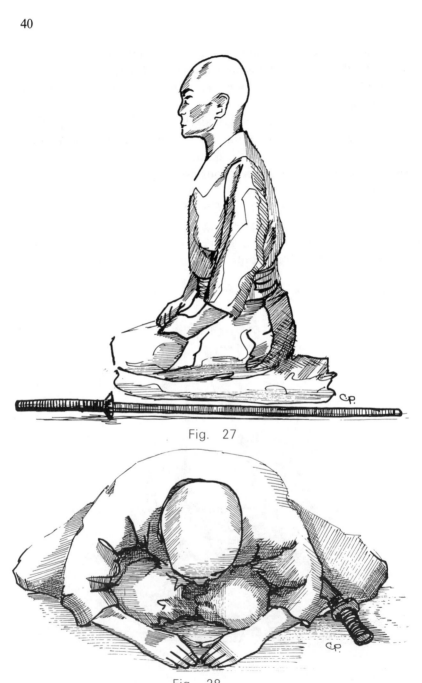

Fig. 27

Fig. 28

and quietly return the right hand and then the left hand to the thighs. At this time you will again be in Seiza.

Now take the left hand and grasp the saya just below the tsuba with your thumb on the tsuba and bring the katana to the left thigh. (See Figure #29.)

Fig. 29

Rise on the back of your feet by going straight up; push up with your thighs but do not lean forward. With your toes under the balls of your feet, you will be in a half-sitting position. Place the right foot against the inside of the left knee and stand erect. (See Figure #30.)

Be sure not to bend the waist while standing up. Align the left foot with the right foot.

Fig. 30

Sitting with Raised Knee: Iai-Hiza

If you are standing with the katana in your obi or belt, this is formally called Taito-shisei. From Taito-shisei you can go into Iai-Hiza. First, place your left thumb on the tsuba, keeping the left forearm next to your hip. Next, start to kneel, taking your right hand and placing the loose part of your hakama in back of your left

Fig. 31

knee. Now touch the left knee to the floor, placing your left foot on the floor so that you can sit on it with your right knee still raised. (See Figures #31 & 32.)

Now sit down: the left heel should be in the center of your body with the instep flat on the floor. You must keep your back and neck straight with the right hand on the right thigh and remain relaxed. While sitting on your left heel, let your right knee slant outwards about fortyfive degrees. Pull the right heel in towards your left knee. Now place both hands on your upper thighs.

Fig. 32

Preparation for Iai-do Practice

You must rememember the Samurai of old Japan believed the highest level of Iai was Saya-no-unchi or invincibility without drawing the sword. So you might say greater than techniques is spiritual training. I believe Iai is a spiritual thing. You must learn to cut the enemy within yourself. If you can accomplish this, you will truly be on your way in Iai. This reminds me of a story of Saya-no-unchi:

One of Japan's greatest swordsman was Tsukahara Bokuden (1490–1572), who had a great depth into Saya-no-unchi. When Bokuden was crossing Beira in a rowboat, with a number of passengers there was braggart among them, a rough-looking Samurai, stalwart and arrogant in every possible way. He boasted of his skill in swordmanship, saying that he was the foremost man in the art. The fellow passengers were eagerly listening to his blatant talk, while Bokuden was dozing as if nothing were going on about him. This irritated the braggart very much. He approached Bokuden and shook him saying, "You also carry a pair of swords, why not say a word?" Bokuden answered quietly, "My art is different from yours; it consists not of defeating others, but in not being defeated." This incensed the fellow immensely. "What is your school then?" "Mine is known as the mutekatsu school (which means to defeat the enemy without hands, that is, without using a sword)". "Why, then, do you yourself carry a sword?" asked the Samurai. "This is meant to do away with selfish motives and not to kill others", answered Bokuden. The man's anger knew no bounds, and he exclaimed in a most impassioned manner, "Do you really mean to fight me with no swords?" "Why not?" was Bokuden's answer. The braggart Samurai called out to the boatman to row toward the nearest land. But Bokuden suggested that it would be better to go to the island farther off because the mainland might attract people who might some how get hurt.

The samurai agreed. The boat headed toward the solitary island at some distance. As soon as they were near enough, the man jumped off the boat and drawing his sword, was all ready for combat. Bokuden leisurely took off his own swords and handed them to the boatman. To all appearance he was about to follow the Samurai onto the island, when Bokuden suddenly took the oar away from the boatman and pushing it against the land, gave a hard backstroke to the boat. There upon, the boat made a precipitous departure from the island and plunged into the deeper water safely away from the man. Bokuden smilingly remarked 'This is my 'No Sword School' ".[1]

Through this story of Bokuden, I feel you can learn to defeat the enemy through his psychological weakness. The worst enemy each of us has is the one only we know about, the one inside of us. This is truly the Samurai's way of Iai.

[1]ibid pp 74–75

Fig. 33

In preparing to practice Iai-do, you must first bow to the sword. After you are in the dojo and have bowed formally to the shrine or to the flag, take your practice position. (See Figure #33.)

You must sit with the shrine or flag on your left. While the left hand holds the katana, place the right hand on your left thigh. The ha is pointing up. With the left thumb on the tsuba, bring the katana forward and across the body. Reaching with the right hand, take hold of the saya just below the tsuba on the koikuchi with both thumbs on the tsuba. Now hold the sword guard between the right index and middle fingers. Pulling the katana to the right across the body, let the saya slide through your left hand between your hip and your thigh. (See Figure #34.)

Stop the saya in the left hand about five inches from the kojiri or end of the saya.

Fig. 34

Now, with both hands, place the katana on the floor in front of you with the cutting edge away from you. Note to be sure to bring the end of the saya slightly to you and away from the shrine or flag. (See Figure #35.)

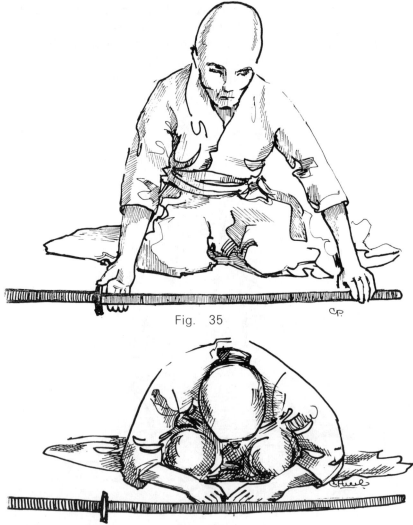

Fig. 35

Fig. 36

Position your hands as in Figure #*36*, bow.

Again, count to five slowly. Do not pop up after the bow but come up slowly. It might be good to note at this time that if you are in a formal class with a sensei or teacher, you should always raise your head only after he has his up. This is very important. Your head should always be a little lower than the sensei's when bowing.

You must now sit in the seiza position and close your eyes trying to reach spiritual preparation with your sword, readying yourself for action. This is called Zanshin and is very important to a true student of Iai-do. You must try and become one with your sword, thinking of it as a part of your body and not a weapon in your hand. Only when you can achieve this frame of mind will you be

Fig. 36A

able to do Iai-do smoothly and find that the significance of Iai is peace and harmony with the universe.

Having completed Zanshin, lean forward, trying to keep your back and head as straight as possible. Place your right hand just below the tsuba on the koikuchi with the thumb holding the tsuba. Your left hand will hold the end of the saya about four inches from the end. (See Figure #35.) Lifting the katana to the right and holding the tsuba with your index finger, insert the katana in your obi or inner-sash. (See. Figures #36 and 36A.)

The katana is now secured. Note, if your katana has a sageo and you are not using it to tie back your sleeves, it is proper at this time to take the sageo in your right hand and bring it across the body to

Fig. 36B

your right side, taking the ends and looping them through your obi or intersash. Make sure you do not pull the sageo tight; it must be very loose. Tie the ends to the obi. Again I must point out there are many different ways to secure the sageo according to the Ryu. Now return the saya. With the Katana secured, align the tsuba with your navel. (See Figure #*36B*.)

Dattao
Removing the Katana from the Obi

Remember that the end of practicing Iai-do is as important as the beginning and each move must be done as flowingly as a bird about

Fig. 37

Fig. 37A

to land on a pond of water. Holding the saya just below the tsuba with the right hand and pressing the tsuba with your thumb, slide the sword out of the obi to your right front. (See Figures #37 and 37A.)

Removing the katana, be sure to let the left hand slide along the saya and stay at the hip. The ha faces your body. Slowly lay the katana down in front of you. (See Figures #38 and 39.)

The ha is toward the left. Your left hand stays on your hip and back. The back and neck remain straight. At this time, replace both hands on your thighs. (See Figure #40.)

Make your bow to the katana, returning your hands to the thighs. (See Figure #41.) Resume Seiza and prepare for Taijo.

Fig. 38

Fig. 39

Fig.   40

Fig.   41

Taijo
Procedure for Leaving the Practice Area

Keeping the left hand on the left thigh, grasp the saya with the right hand just below the tsuba. (Keep the index finger on the tsuba). Now raise the katana to a vertical position. (See Figure #42.)

The ha should be toward you and the katana should be in the center of your knees about one foot forward. Now put your left

Fig. 42

hand around the saya and gently slide the hand down to the end of the saya. (See Figure #43.)

Lift the katana and place it on your lap with the end of the saya pointing to the rear.(See Figure #44.)

Now, quietly move the right leg forward and assume the formal stance. After you have stood up, take three steps backward. Turning to the place of honor, the shrine, or the flag, put the katana in the right hand and bow. Then return the katana to the left hand and leave the practice area. Note that if you have a teacher present, it would be proper to go to him at this time and bow. Do not carry

Fig. 43

your katana with you. When you have mastered all these things, you will be ready to start your lessons in drawing the sword from the saya.

Fig. 44

CHAPTER FOUR

Fuwa Kazuemon Masatane   (Ronin of AKO)

Nukikata, Drawing of the Sword

Kata Number One
Ippon Me Mae

MIND LIKE WATER

A reflection in water is the symbol of a
clear, calm mind in harmony with its
surrounding—the highest level of
training in a martial art.

Before we actually draw the sword, let me put you in the right
frame of mind. I have previously said you should try to empty your
mind of the day's thoughts. Close your eyes, think of something
pleasant, something that has happened or that you wish would
happen. Let your shoulders relax. It is most important to be relaxed
before and during practice. Remember that if you throw a rock in a
pond, it makes a splash for only a second and then every drop of
water returns to its previous stillness, as nothing had happened.
This is most important. The draw must appear out of nowhere, in
effect, "Now you see it, now you don't." I do not want you to think
this is done by a trick or by speed; it is something very hard to
explain. The best way I know to explain the appearance of the
katana in Iai is to compare it with hunting. Have you ever been
hunting or deep in a forest sitting very quietly? Everything stops
and you can hear a pin drop. The noise of the forest starts up again,
everything is as it was with you as quiet and relaxed as possible.
You can see nothing unusual, your eyes look all around and out of
nowhere a deer or small animal appears, as if it had just materia-
lized from thin air. Now this is Iai—The movement becomes so
natural that the sword just seems to materialize from your hand.

Fig. 45

There is no jerking movement, nothing out of the ordinary to catch the eye—except that the first time they looked the sword was not in your hand and the next second it was. The first reaction people seem to have to this is, "How did you do that?" A question that is impossible to answer.

Attain the seiza position by kneeling with the knees eight or so inches apart, place the big toes flat on the floor, and sit on your heels with your hands on your thighs. (See Figure #45.)

This kata starts as you sense the enemy about to attack you. You will cut his right temple just above the ear and then deliver the finishing cut of a downward stroke. This kata, as with all katas, starts with a breathing exercise. Take three deep breaths, letting each one half way out and then the rest. Now repeat this action, only this time—on the last breath— inhale and while drawing the blade, exhale. Now put your left hand on the Koikuchi with the thumb on the tsuba and bring the end of the saya across your body. The tsuba or handle should be within reach of your right hand. Note that you do not reach across your body with your right hand to take hold of the handle. The reason for this is quite simple, in that you will expose your right kote (or wrist) to your opponent for a downward cut. Next, take the tsuba in your right hand and push with your left thumb against the tsuba, so that the blade has slipped out of the saya about one half inch. At this time, push up with your legs, using mostly your thigh muscles. This motion will bring your body straight up instead of leaning forward with your head down exposing your neck to your opponent. When you have attained about one half of your height, bring your toes under your feet so that the balls of your feet are on the floor. Now, turn the saya so that the cutting edge of the katana is away from your body. This is

Fig. 46

done by giving the saya a half twist with your left hand by using the wrist only. Keep your head straight and your eyes about four or five feet on the floor in front of you. Next, pull the blade out of the saya except for two or three inches. (See Figure #46.)

Now as you pull the remaining three to four inches of the blade out of the saya, bring your right foot out in front of you making a 90° angle with your thigh and the calf of your right leg. This is a horizontal cut. (See Figure #47.)

You should stamp the floor as the sword comes to a stop so that the body and the sword end the movement at the same time.

Note that your left shoulder should be pulled back slightly and your rear foot should have only the ball on the floor. For a rear view of this see Figure #47A.

Another point to keep in mind while making this cut is that you

Fig. 47

should pull the end of the saya (koikuchi) away from your body so that the Kojiri or tip of the saya is even with your right knee. (See Figure #48.)

Again, do not be too anxious to do the next movement until you have studied these three previous drawings carefully. (Refer back to Figures #46, 47.) As you see in Figure #48, the correct movement in holding the Kuchi is that the little finger should be on the obi and the elbow should be pulled to the rear. This movement is called

Fig. 47A

sayabiki or saya pulling. Figure #49 points out that the wrist should not be bent and Figure #50 points out that the little finger is not touching the obi. It also points out that the wrist does not touch the waist, which would be incorrect.

Fig. 48

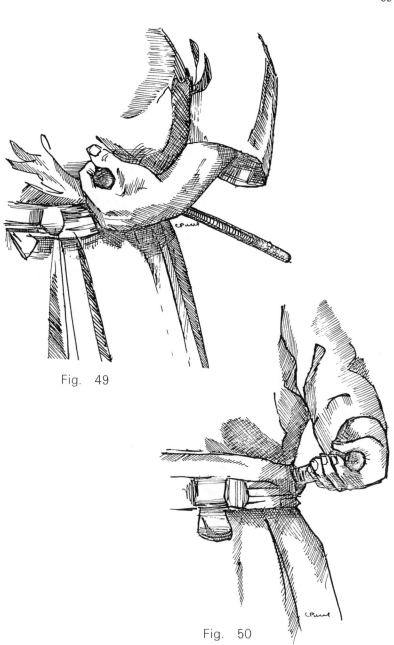

Fig. 49

Fig. 50

If you have studied these last movements in depth, you are now ready to start the killing blow or the downward cut. Figure *#51* illustrates how to bring the katana around to the left side of the head, keeping the blade straight and the cutting edge away from you.

The wrist should not be bent. Next, take a step with your left knee, and by pushing with the ball of your left foot, align your left knee with the heel of your right foot. This action is done by keeping a low profile. Do not raise and lower your body. Now, raise the katana above your head quickly, but not in a jerking movement and take hold of the handle with the left hand. (See Figure *#52*.)

The hands and the sword should be in the direct center of your body and the blade should be vertical. Note that some Ryu teach letting the back or shinogi of the blade touch the back to make this cut. If you do practice this cut that way, you will develop a stronger cut, but with a slower movement. I find it very helpful to practice

Fig. 51

these movements in a mirror so that incorrect technique can easily be seen.

As you pull the blade forward, making a circle over your head, bring the right foot forward and stamp the foot at the same time you complete your cut. (See Figure #53.)

Keep your back and head straight. Do not lock your elbows. The body should have moved forward about one and a half feet, and the

Fig. 52

blade will be at a 45° angle. The tsukagashira of the handle will be pointing at your navel. To complete this cut, stop the katana with the tsukagashira of the handle still pointing at the navel and the end of the blade about one foot from the floor. The hand movements for this and all two handed cuts will be like wringing out a wet towel; right and left hands twisting inward to the center of the handle. Your hands should be on the menukis of the handle. You have now completed the cutting action of this kata. (See Figure #54.)

Your next movement will be the chiburi or removing the blood from the blade. (See Figure #55.)

Fig. 53

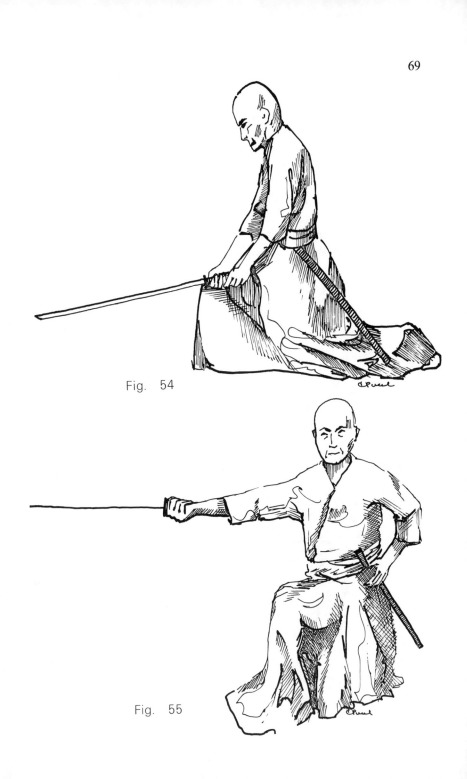

Fig. 54

Fig. 55

Place your left hand on the saya, and push the sword a little forward turning the cutting edge to your right and bringing the sword up to the right side of the body with the blade horizontal and with the elbow slightly bent. Now bring the katana up close to the top of your ear (this is done by just bending the elbow). (See Figure #56.)

While keeping your back and head straight, simultaneously rise to your feet and make a circle over your head. Stop the blade about 40° downward and even with your right knee. This action should be done with the knees spread slightly outward and sinking at the

Fig. 56

Fig. 57

waist. The right and left hand should be on the same line and your eyes focused five or six feet in front of you. (See Figure #57.) Note that the movement of shaking the blood off of the katana is like popping a whip and is mostly a wrist action technique.

Now, bring the left foot up even with the front right foot. Stay in a squatting position and do not allow your body to move up and down. (See Figure #58.)

Fig.　58

Holding this squatting position with the knees bent just a little, bring the right foot to the rear. (See Figure #59.) Note that the rest of your body does not move from its previous position.

Figure #60 illustrates the starting movements for the blade's return to the saya: move the left hand and place it around the opening of the saya turning the saya sideways in your obi using the middle finger and thumb. Place the back of the blade about where the mune is between your left index finger and thumb. Note that if you are using a real sword to be extremembly careful at this point so that you do not cut your thumb on the return of the blade.

Fig. 59

Now, slide the blade out to the very tip holding it still with only your forefinger and thumb. When you feel the end (kissaki) of the blade reach the opening of the saya (koikuchi), start to push back so that the blade will start on its way into the saya, you will have to release your grip on the handle just a little holding the handle (tsuka) with your fingers and thumb. Remember to keep your back and head straight, looking ahead and keep your knees bent. (See Figure #61.)

Fig. 60

It should be mentioned here that it would be best to look down at the saya a few times till you get the feel of this movement. Always remember a true Iaiest never looks down on the return because the sword and you are one. You do not look down when you put your hand in your pocket, do you?

Simultaneously slide the saya to the tsuba and the blade in the saya. Turn the saya up so that the cutting edge is pointing upwards. All this is done while you are lowering your right knee to the floor. Keeping your back and neck straight, tilt your head just a little and

Fig. 61

focus your eyes on a spot ahead of you. When the tsuka has reached the koikuchi, slide the katana back in your obi or belt just a little by placing your left thumb on the tsuba. (See Figure #62.)

When you have completed this movement, rise to your feet, pushing up with the ball of your rear foot. When you stand up do not lean forward, but go straight upward. Now, align your front foot with your back foot by stepping back with your left foot. Replace your right hand to your side and assume taito-shisei position. (See Figure #63.)

Fig. 62

Fig. 63

This completes the first Kata: Ippon Me Mae. This kata should be practiced at least five hundred times before proceeding to the next kata. Keep in mind all the small movements it requires as you would keep in mind all the ingredients necessary to make a good stew.

Kata Number Two
Nihon Me Ushiro

Isogai Jurozaemon Masahisa (Ronin of AKO)

Nihon Me Ushiro or attacking from behind to the front begins with the seiza position. (See Figure #64.)

Remember that the kata starts with your hands on your thighs and the tsuba of the katana even with your navel or the center of your body. Note that as you start this kata, your back is to the flag or the shrine. Your big toes are touching and the tops of your feet are flat on the floor. (See Figure #64–A.)

The movement of this kata occurs when the enemy is behind you; you will make a 180° turn to the rear and cut his right temple.

As you begin to raise your body using your thigh muscles, turn the katana sideways with the cutting edge away from you and

Fig. 64

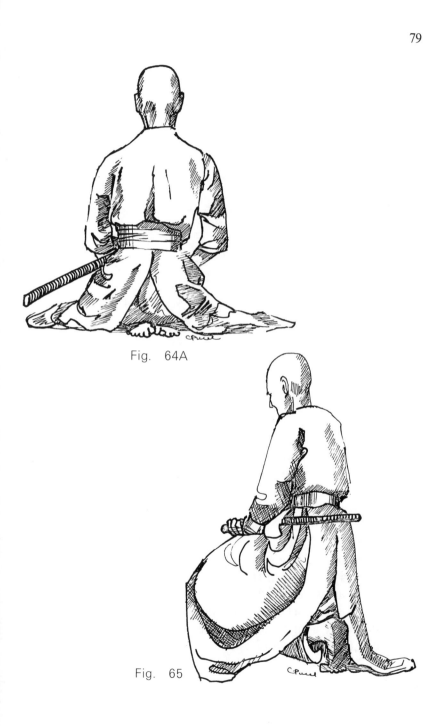

Fig. 64A

Fig. 65

Fig. 66

slowly start the blade out of the saya. Now bring the toes under the ball of the right foot and start the left leg up, turning 180° to the left by pivoting on the right knee. (See Figure #65.)

You are now facing the front of the enemy. Stamp the left foot on the floor as you complete this horizontal cut, cutting the enemy on the right temple.(See Figure #66.)

Now complete the other thirteen movements as in kata number one. Everything remains the same except that the foot movement is reversed.

Remember:

> Our brains are given to us as instruments capable of a specific, a limited task. When trying to understand the real mysteries, the brain stops short. The brain can contain neither the questions themselves, nor the answers. To come to real under-standing, to enlightenment, quite another instrument has to be used, intuitive insight.[1]

[1]Van de Wetering, J. *The Empty Mirror* (Boston: The Houghton Mifflin Co.), p. 8 and 9

Kata Number Three
Ukenagashi
(Warding off)

Horibe Yahyoe Kanemaru (Ronin of AKO)

82

By the time a student encounters the third kata, he should be discovering that Iai-do is an art and like many other arts in Japan it is seen as a way of enlightenment. The technical training of stances, cuts, blocks, etc. must be combined with the spiritual training of the "way" if the ultimate goal of Iai-do is to be reached: the sword of no sword. From the viewpoint of purely technical skill, the beginner and master are the same. All knowledge is a circle, for both the master and the beginner move instinctively, without any cognition between perception and correct response. Once the first technique is learned then the student is no longer a beginner and he is on the way. He must either continue to travel the circular path that is the way or he finds that he would have been better off if he had never learned his first technique.

In this kata, Ukenagashi, the enemy is to your left and he

Fig.   67

suddenly attacks you. Starting from seiza, remove your hands from your thighs and place them on your katana as in kata number two. Do not forget to push the tsuba with your thumb. Rise straight up, using your thigh muscles, but tilting your body just a little forward about twenty degrees and to the right. Turning the upper part of your body and head to face the attacker, start your draw. The cutting edge of your blade is upward. (See Figure #67.)

Draw the blade out close to your chest and then raise it over the head slanting the tip downward about 35 degrees to ward off the opponent's attack. This movement is done with the left foot forward. (See Figure #68.)

Fig. 68

Now, standing up, right foot to the rear, keeping the knees bent, bring the right foot to the heel of the left foot. The left heel should be turned outward. (See Figure #69.)

You have blocked the enemy's sword. Step to the rear with the left foot turning about 90 degrees to your left facing your enemy. This turning movement is done when you have taken hold of the handle of your sword with both hands and delivered a downward stroke to the enemy's left shoulder. The downward stroke stops with the tsuka at the middle of your waist and the tip about even with the middle of your stomach. The cutting edge of the blade should be angled to the left just a little. (See Figure #70.)

Fig. 69   Fig. 70

While holding this position, bend your front knee a little, which in this case is your right knee. Bring the handle up and to the left side of your body and slightly release the grip with your right hand. Then place the end of the blade about six inches up from the knee on your right leg. (See Figure #71.)

The right hand should be next to the tsuba with the hand open, but holding the handle between the thumb and index finger.

At this time regrip the handle as in Figure #72, turning the right hand over.

Hold the handle firmly with your left hand, but only with the fingers and thumb of your right. You must be ready at anytime for the enemy's possible counterattack.

Fig. 71   Fig. 72

Next, while still keeping your eyes on the opponent, remove your left hand from the handle and take hold of the opening of the saya making ready for the return. (See Figure #73.)

Holding the handle of the sword with your fingers and thumb of your right hand, bring the back of the blade to the left hand. Note that you should place the back of the blade between the thumb and the index finger of the left hand about midway down from the tsuba. (See Figure #74.)

The tip of the blade will be pointing to the rear with the cutting edge away from your body.

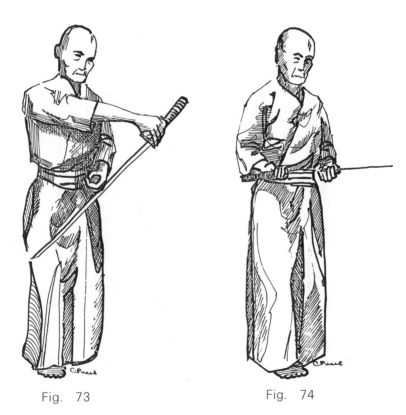

Fig. 73   Fig. 74

Start pulling the back of the blade between your left index finger and thumb. Bring the handle out and to the left of your body. When you feel the kissaki or tip of the blade between your thumb and finger, place it in the koikuchi of the saya. Start the return. Note that the blade is still turned with the cutting edge away from you. This movement is executed while you are bending the left knee. When your left knee is about half way from the floor, turn the saya upward so that the cutting edge is now up and you are letting the blade ride on the mune. Continue down till the left knee touches the floor. The movement of the blade and the knee end at the same time. (See Figure #75.)

Fig. 75

Using the ball of the left foot and the right thigh muscles rise to your feet. Bring the left foot to the right foot. Note that when rising you do not lean forward but come straight up, keeping your eyes on the opponent or on the floor five to six feet in front of you. After aligning your feet, take your right hand off of the handle and bring it to your side. Place your left thumb on the tsuba and assume the taito shisei. (See Figure #76.)

Fig. 76

CHAPTER FIVE

Chiba Saburobei Mitsutada   (Ronin of AKO)

Seppuku (Abdomen Cutting)

In recent decades Japan's legends and feudal practices have become familiar to many of us. By far the most talked about is seppuku. When you read something about one cutting himself open, somehow the mind always goes back to the Japanese and asks the question, "Why would anyone do such a thing?" First, I think you would have to be Japanese to understand. Many books and endless talking to some of the old Japanese masters have made me understand the Japanese feeling about the subject. But I must confess I do not understand how men could do such a thing in the frame of mind in which they did it.

Many Westerners with whom I've discussed the subject seem to feel that the act of seppuku was committed in a drugged or drunken state. To be sure you understand seppuku or hara-kiri (abdomen cutting), let me make this clear; At no time were those men committing seppuku under the influence of any drugs or drink. On the contrary, their minds were as clear as crystal and knew what they were doing every minute. Seppuku, the formal name, and hara-kiri, the more common word for the practice, go back in Japanese history to about A. D. 1336. Before this time, it was the custom in crimes deserving capital punishment to either behead or to strangle the condemned person not much different than the European custom of hanging or the French custom of using the guillotine. (And I might add, preferable to being burned at the stake or being stoned to death by a mob.) I am not suggesting that seppuku was a pleasant way to die, but for the Japanese it was a way for them to die with honor and self-respect, and to keep their name clean.

Today most of us feel that there is no particularly "good" way of putting an end to one's life, but if you were born a warrior, or Samurai, in Japan, the way you died was very important to you and your family. I think elements of the same sentiment are evident even in our society today. If a member of your family committed a capital crime and was executed, you would be reluctant to discuss the death socially. On the other hand, if the relative committed suicide in a very brave and dramatic way before being arrested for his offense, his death tends to elicit social compassion and sympathy rather than the disdain shown a convicted murderer.

During the period of time in Japan's history that seppuku was customary, only samurai were allowed to practice this manner of suicide. The act of seppuku had as many formalitites as would a White House State Dinner for visiting nobility.

The samurai was well trained in the ceremony of seppuku because he might have to take a role in it or at least might have to teach it to younger samurai just beginning their journey as warriors. First, it was necessary to select witnesses, then find a place for the condemned man to wait. Next, a location for the ceremony had to be determined and then seconds had to be selected. A second was one of the most important men in the ceremony; he had to be chosen very carefully and usually agreed to by the condemned man. A samurai who acted as a second was called kaishaku. The kaishaku was required to be of sound mind and body. He was to show neither his like nor dislike for the office given him. The kaishaku wore a formal dress called hempen, with the hakama tucked under the belt. In the ceremony, he must not wear his sword, but should have a small knife hidden upon him somewhere. There were three seconds in the ceremony, the head kaishaku, his assistant and a lower class kaishaku. It is the duty of the head second to cut off the condemned man's head and this is the most important position in the ceremony of seppuku. The assistant kaishaku handles the tray upon which the small knife with which the condemned man cuts himself open is placed. The third kaishaku carries the severed head to the witnesses for identification. The third man is also important because he might be called upon to cut off the head if something should happen to the other two men.

It is very interesting to note that the second who cuts off the head is not allowed to use his own sword, but must use the condemned man's own weapon. The reason for this being if a mishap in the beheading occurs, it can be blamed on the victim's sword and not the kaishaku. It is the second's job to decapitate the condemned man with a single blow. You might think this a simple thing to do, especially for a samurai trained to use the sword almost from the time he could walk, but let me add one further point: the head had to be cut off, except for a little piece of skin which was to keep the head from falling off the platform and touching the ground. To cut off a man's head this way, the samurai had to know precisely what he was doing and have extraordinary control. He and his sword had to be as one.

When all was prepared for the ceremony of seppuku and the condemned man had bathed, fixed his hair, put on his white formal clothes, and said his good-byes to his close friends, he was lead out to the mats where the ceremony was to take place. (See Figure #77.)

Fig. 77

At this time, according to his rank, he might ask for a pen and paper to write his farewells. This was kept to an acceptable minimum of time. The second should be to the left and out of sight of the condemned man. The condemned man faced west and the second faced the north. When the condemned man had put his writing implements down, the second made himself ready. The condemned man at this time stripped himself from the waist down, tucking his upper clothing under his knees and legs tightly so as to support his body. This was done so his body would fall forward

Fig. 78

and not backward. At this time the condemned man reached out and grasped the dirk or small knife. Pointing the dirk to himself and inserting it in his stomach with both hands, he drew it across his stomach from left to right, twisting the knife and pulling it up to the solar plexus, by following the lower rib. This done, he withdraw the dirk and laid it down. Not a sound is to be heard from the condemned man or anyone else at the ceremony. (See Figure #78.)

The second then stepped to the left and placed himself in position to strike the final blow. The condemned man leaned forward and extended his neck. The kaishaku who has followed every movemant of the condemned man, now without delay, raises his katana and with the speed of lightning removes the head from the body (all but a tiny piece of skin under the chin). If this is accomplished, the kaishaku has done his job well. (See Figure #79.)

Fig. 79

Note: Laying down thick paper and placing the head on it shows a disposition to pay respect to the head; to place in on the edge of the sword is insulting: the course pursued must depend upon the rank of the person. If the ceremony is to be curtailed, it may end with the cutting off of the head; that must be settled beforehand, in a consultation with the witnesses. In the event of the second making a false cut, so as not to strike off the head at a blow, he must take the head by the top knot, press it down, and cut it off. Should he take poor aim and cut into the shoulder by mistake and should the principal rise and cry out, before he has time to writhe, he should hold him down and stab him to death, and then cut off his head, or the assistant seconds, who are sitting behind, should come forward and hold him down, while the chief second cuts off the head. It may be necessary for the second, after he has cut off the head, to push down the body, and then pick up the head for inspection. If the body does not fall at once, which is said to be sometimes the case, the second should pull the feet to make it fall.[1]

[1]A. B. Mitford (Lord Redesdale) *Tales of Old Japan* (Charles E. Tuttle Co, Inc., Appendix A., An account of the Hara-Kiri, from a rare Japanese MS, Third Printing) 1970. pp. 398

CHAPTER SIX

Ohishi Chikara Yoshikane   (Ronin of AKO)

Iai-Hiza Division

Kata Number Four
Tsuka-Ate

This kata starts with you sitting in the Iai-hiza position. (See Page #69 for further information on Iai-hiza.) When you are threatened from the front and rear, Tsuka-ate could be applied. This consists of striking the front attacker with the end of the handle in the solar plexus, thrusting at the rear attacker with the blade and then finishing off the front attacker with a downward cut.

With this kata you are confronted with two attackers, and the most important thing to remember is not to let your mind dwell on any one object or on the movement of the attackers.

For instance, suppose ten men are opposing you, each in succession ready to attack you with a sword. As soon as one is disposed of, you will move on to another without permitting the mind to stop with any action. However rapidly one blow may follow another you leave no time to intervene between the two. Every one of the ten will thus be successively and successfully dealt with. This is possible only when the mind moves from one object to another without being "stopped" or arrested by anything. If the mind is unable to move on in this fashion, it is sure to lose the game somewhere between two encounters.[1]

To expand on mind-stopping would take a book in itself and I am by no means a Zen master able to teach these things. As my Master once told me, I can only show you the way, I cannot teach you; you must teach yourself. As I have told you before, you must become one with your sword. Before you attempt this kata though, I want you to think about what I have said: Do not be like so many other people who read the beginning, the middle, and the end of a book and then tell everyone how wonderful or how terrible it was.

To state it in terms of swordmanship, the genuine beginner

[1]Ibid pp. 98

knows nothing about the way of holding and managing the sword, and much less of his concern for himself. When the opponent tries to strike him, he instinctively parries it. This is all he can do. But, as soon as the training starts, he is taught how to handle the sword, where to keep the mind, and many other technical tricks—which makes his mind "stop" at various junctures. For this reason whenever he tries to strike the opponent he feels unusually hampered: (He has lost altogether the original sense of innocence and freedom). But as days and years go by, as his training acquires fuller maturity, his bodily attitude and his way of managing the sword advance toward 'No-Mind-ness' which resembles the state of mind he had at the very beginning of training when he knew nothing, when he was altogether ignorant of the art. The beginning and the end thus turn into next-door neighbors. First, we start counting one, two, three, and when finally ten is counted, we return to one.[2]

[2]Ibid pp. 99–100

Fig. 80

You must believe me when I tell you that there are no short cuts in Iai-do. Each person entering into the art must labor in slow pain like a mother giving birth. Only after the birth of her child, can she explain the highs and lows of it.

Figure #80 illustrates sitting in Iai-Hiza.

As you are facing the shrine, place both hands on the katana with the right hand on the handle and the left hand on the saya. Do not push the tsuba with your thumb. Pushing up with the side of the right foot and lifting upward with the thigh of the left leg, rise to your left knee. Stamp the right foot on the floor as you bring the katana and saya forward to strike the enemy in front of you with the end of the handle of your katana. Note that the end of the handle, the tsukagashira, will be extended at arms length and even with your own solar plexus. (See Figure #81.)

Fig. 81

Fig. 82

Fig. 83

Now, pull the saya back with your left hand to your obi, and continue pulling the katana out of the saya with your left hand. You body should be centered with your left knee and the top of your body leaning to the left at 40–45°. (See Figure #82.)

You now see the enemy behind you, and the katana has cleared the saya. Turn the handle so that the cutting edge of the blade is away from you and so that the katana is horizontal with the floor. It should also be half way between your solar plexus and your waist, close to your chest. (See Figure #83.)

Now, without changing your position, extend the right elbow and thrust to the enemy's solar plexus. Keep your back and head straight. Do not allow yourself to slump in this movement. (See Figure #84.)

Fig. 84

Fig. 85

Fig. 86

Pulling the katana over your head, take hold of the handle with the left hand. Turn your body back to the front and deliver a downward cut to your first opponent. (See Figure #85.)

While remaining in this position, execute Chiburi (or shaking off the blood). This is done on the right side. Be sure to keep your left palm on your hip.

While you are holding the downward cut, let go of the handle with your left hand replacing it on your waist and with your right hand bring the blade to your right side with the cutting edge away from you. The blade should be even with your right knee, but at arm's length, with the wrist bent upward slightly and the kissaki lowered. (See Figure #86.)

Move the katana slightly forward, turning the blade edge to the left. Next, raise the sword from the floor even with your shoulder

Fig. 87

with the kissaki away from you. The elbow is slightly turned toward the inside. Now, bending your elbow so that the tsuba is about one and one half inches from your temple, arc the blade over your head and stop in the same position in which you started the movement. (See Figure #86 again.)

To return the katana to the saya, place your left hand around the koikuchi of the saya and bring the hand to your navel. Place the back of the blade between your thumb and index finger about three inches from the kissaki. Now, pull the blade outward until you feel the tip in your thumb and finger. Remember to keep your back straight and your eyes on the floor in front of you. Now, start the return. (See Figure #87.)

As you are returning the blade to the saya, slide the right foot to the rear and align it with your left. Do not raise the body in this movement. With the feet aligned, you will be sitting on the heel of your left foot with the ball of the foot on the floor. The left knee will

Fig. 88

slowly decline to the floor and the right knee will be 90° to the right. Your thighs will be forming an "L" shape. The ball of the right foot will be on the floor. (See Figure #88.)

Now, with your left thumb on the tsuba, bring your right knee to the front. Next, with the tsuba in the center of your body, rise to the standing position (taito shisei). Align the rear foot with the front and remove the right hand from the handle.

This is the last of the sitting katas in this Ryu. But always remember that the last of one thing is the beginning of another. Be sure you know where you have been so that you can return, before you start out for places unknown.

When the sword is in the hands of a technician swordsman skilled in its use, it is no more than an instrument with no mind of its own. What it does is done mechanically, and there is no myōyū discernible in it. But, when the sword is held by the swordsman whose spiritual attainment is such that he holds it as though not holding it, it is identified with the man himself, it acquires a soul, it moves with all the subtleties which have been imbedded in him as a swordsman. The man emptied of all thoughts, all emotions originating from fear, all sense of insecurity, all desire to win, is not conscious of using the sword; both man and sword turn into instruments in the hands, as it were, of the unconscious, and it is this unconscious that achieves wonders of creativity. It is here that swordplay becomes an art.[3]

---

[3]Ibid, pp. 146

CHAPTER SEVEN

Hazama Shinroku Mitsukaze   (Ronin)

Happo-no-Kamae

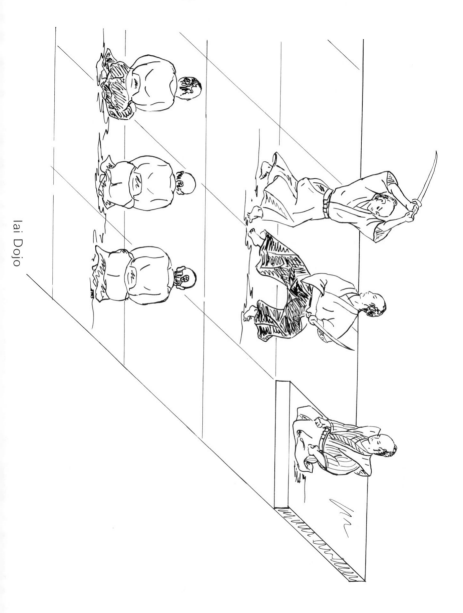

Iai Dojo

不然乎

刉不失洪王五右手如小臂大豈

為人叙之若推而上之則准降長

是非尚之非幻之左幾逞可以學

捄玫則玫可韶一刉不蔡二刀誠

捣辰仲世真得于心膣于手挈則

曰二刀流其两挈西义措狄横抑

刿客斯克玄信每一手持一刀擔

袖衷青蛇菀下者方士之幻術之

攷氏打連抹打者果愍之妛籯之

Fig. 89

"It is absurd to generate a tornado with bare hands. It is also magic to throw a dagger from underneath sleeves. The sword man, Genshin Shinmen, claims that, if you can handle two swords (one in each hand) with perfect control, then you are able to beat your opponent who holds one sword. This is not absurd nor magic.
He also says that, if you keep on learning the way of two swords, you will be as good as an imperial guard of Han.*

As I have stated before, drawing the sword out of the saya is Iai, but once it has been taken out of its resting place, you have

*Han: A Chinese dynasty dated 207 B.C.-A.D. 220 and marked by centralized control through an appointive bureaucracy, a revival of learning, and the penetration of Buddhism. (Webster's dictionary)

Kenjutsu or Kendo offensive swordsmanship. In this chapter I would like to talk about Happo-no-Kamae and Happo-Giri. Happo-no-Kamae translated means "style of eight directions" and Happo-Giri means "cutting style of eight directions." In a self portrait of Miyamoto Musashi (See Figure #89), he holds his swords in a ready position known as "Happo-Biraki," or "open on all eight sides." It was believed that with this on-guard position there were no possible openings for attack. No book on swordmanship would be complete without mentioning the greatest swordman

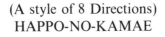

(A style of 8 Directions)
HAPPO-NO-KAMAE

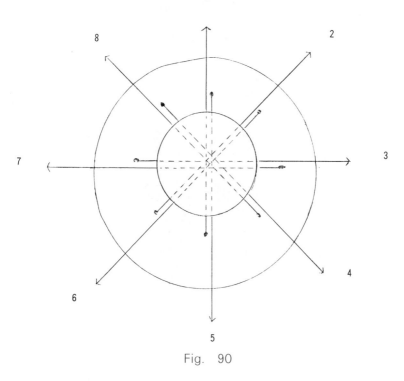

Fig. 90

of his time, Master Miyamoto Musashi (Kensei), "Sword Saint" of Kenjutsu. Master Musashi was born in a Japanese village called Miyamoto in the province of Mimashaka in 1584 on the outskirts of Edo or present-day Tokyo. He died in a cave, where he lived alone for the last two years of his life, in May of 1645, leaving his famous book "Five Rings" to his ken students. It is said that his book explaining the sword and life itself is still used by businessmen

7 ←   → 3

Fig. 90A

in Japan today. If only half the things that I have heard and read about him are true, he was a remarkable man indeed. It is said he had over sixty duels before he was twenty-nine years old and won all of them. Imagine discovering an old sword that was made in his era in someone's attic. Who knows, Musashi might even have used

Fig. 90B

it, or fought against the person who did own it. There are no ends to the mysteries of Japanese swords.

I do not know if Musashi was an expert in Iai. In most of the accounts I have read, and in the stories my Kendo teachers in Japan

Fig. 90C

have told me, he is portrayed with his swords out of the saya before the duel. Nevertheless, I know he had to be a master of the arts of Happo-no-Kamae and Happo-Giri. As in Figure #90, & 90ABCD you can see the circle of life with the eight points of directions.

Fig. 90D

These are the same eight points of off-balance every Martial Art uses today. Nothing really changes, does it? Life procedes in a circle till we find the end which only turns out to be the beginning of something new.

If you are standing in the center of this circle and holding your katana in Chudan-no-Kamae or middle readiness, point the kissaki of the blade at your opponent's throat. If you have no opponent, point the kissaki at your own throat. The handle should be about even with your waist and one fist away from your body. For proper handle grip, see the Chapter on sword testing, page #263. Fig 131. The right hand should be forward. Now, not leaving the spot where you are standing, turn slowly 360 degrees, keeping an eye on the kissaki as you move and you will find your circle. This circle is the

Fiqures one through eight.
(A style of 8 Directions)
HAPPO-NO-KAMAE

1. Chudan-no-Kamae
   (Middle)

2. Gedan-no-Kamae
   (Down)

outer perimeter of your defense. Each person's circle is different depending on his build and size. Needless to say, you have the same circle whether you are doing Kendo or Iai-do. You may spend many hours wondering what I am talking about here, but your circle is the most important thing you will ever learn. You must not give up on it, the circle must become a part of you and your sword. Maybe I can explain it this way. You have always had a circle with you; it is the extension of your hand at arms length. When you reach out you never think anything about it, and if the object is just a little out of reach your mind tells you that you have to lean over to get it. This is where most accidents happen; you may lose your balance and sometimes fall. In Kenjutsu, that moment your mind was clouded with the thought of moving, you could be struck

3. Hidari-Jodan-no-Kamae
    (Up Left)

4. Migi-Jodan-no-Kamae
    (Up Right)

5. Hidari-Hassou-no-Kamae
(Left up even with chin)

6. Migi-Hassou-no-Kamae
(Right up even with chin)

7. Hidari Waki-no-Kamae
(Down Left)

8. Migi-Waki-no-Kamae
(Down Right)

down. You must know your circle with your sword as if it were your hand.

Once your opponent has entered your circle with the tip of his sword, he can be cut down. If you look at Figure #90 again, you will find the inner circle where the small line ends is where the cut should occur. In Iai-do, facing to line one, you can cut and block on any of these eight lines. As shown on pages *174 & 175*, Figures *1* through *8*, you can see the different ready positions for on-guard readiness.

Pages #*176–178*, Figures *1* through *8*, demonstrate the eight different cutting styles of the eight directions. These should be studied until they are automatic to the mind.

Happo-Giri

(Cutting-Style of 8 Direction)
Happo-Giri
Hachi-No-Giri

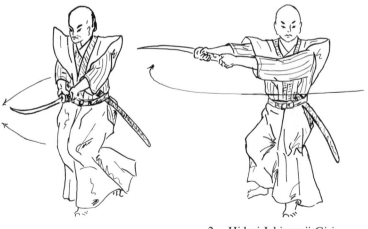

1. Morote-Tsuki
   (Push to the front)

2. Hidari-Ichimonji-Giri
   (Cut horizontally from left side)

3. Migi-Ichimonji-Giri
   (Cut horizontally from
   right side)

4. Suichyoku-Giri
   (Vertically from up
   to down)

5. Hidari-Kesa-Giri
   (Cut down across from
   upper right side)

6. Migi-Kesa-Giri
   (Cut down across from upper
   left side)

7. Hidari-Joho-Giri
   Cut up across from lower
   right side)

8. Migi-Joho-Giri
   (Cut up across from lower
   left side)

CHAPTER EIGHT

Onodera Junai Hidekazu
(Ronin of AKO)

Iai-do Bujitsu

When working with the sword as I have said before, it must become one with you. It must become implanted, as if a working part of your body, in the unconscious mind. To point this out, let me refer to a story that I use in class. Have you ever been engrossed in something, it does not matter what, but deeply involved in your work? Suddenly and unexpectedly someone says something to you. You are startled and jump, raising your hand or hands up to your face for protection. Have you ever asked yourself why you reacted that way? It is your subconscious mind at work. Your subconscious has taken over the movement of your body without the body having any knowledge of it until the movement is finished. The subconscious part of your mind has used your body without letting the brain know about it until the danger has passed. This is how the sword must work in your hand with Iai-do. Your motion must be so smooth that your mind, body and sword all move together. Only the subconscious mind really knows that the sword is not really a part of you.

There are three stages of mind control in swordmanship. There is an ancient story about this. There once lived an old sword master in Kyushu who was about to retire from teaching Kenjutsu. He had three sons and before he retired, he had to select one as his successor. So he invited his best friend to his house to help with the election. Upon the arrival of his friend, as was the custom in those days, he invited him to have a cup of tea. While they were drinking their tea and talking, they decided to play a small game with the three sons as a sort of test of their martial arts training as well as their physical ability. They placed a large heavy pillow above the door to their quarters so that when the door opened the pillow would fall and hit the person who entered. Upon completion of this task they made ready and the father called out to his youngest son to come to his aid. After about two or three minutes with no response, the father called out again, and in a loud voice the son answered, "Just a minute, Father." The father and his guest smiled at each other while sipping their tea. In a few minutes the son came to the door, opened it and stepped in. At the moment he entered the room down came the heavy pillow. But before it could land on his head, the young man jumped aside drawing his sword with lightning speed, cutting the pillow in half. Then after looking all around the room with sword in hand waiting for further action and feeling that the danger had passed, he replaced the sword in the saya and kicked the two halves of the pillow out of the way. He then bowed to the guest and then to his father asking what his father wanted with him. The father introduced him to his best friend saying, "This is my youngest son. As you can see he is as fast as the hunting falcon." Dismissing the youngest son, he instructed him not to say a word about what had happened to his brothers. They then called for the next son. The next oldest son did not respond immediately, but it was not necessary to call him the second time. Arriving at the door, the son knocked and upon hearing his father reply, slid the door open and stepped in. Again, a heavy pillow came crashing down. The young man reached for his sword, but, instead of drawing, he caught the pillow in his hands. Turning his head to his father with a bewildered look, he replaced the pillow above the door. Bowing to his father's friend and then to his father, he asked what service he could be to them? The father introduced him saying, "This is my middle son, he has the eyes and calmness of a tiger before the kill." Instructing this son as the one before, they called for the eldest. Now the oldest son came at once and knocked on the door. The father called to him to enter, but the door did not move. After a second or two the father again bade him enter. This time the oldest son slid the door open about a foot, smiling through the doorway at his father and his father's friend. The son reached up through the doorway, took the pillow down, stepped through the doorway and replaced the pillow above the door. Turning to his father's guest, the son gave him a long and low bow, then turned to his father and also bowed. At this the father remarked to his friend. "This is my son, Kira, he is almost as wise as I. We think we are different only because we agree to think so." The friend bowed to the oldest son and said, "You have learned your lessons very well;

you are surely your father in his youth. Your father has been the needle, and you the thread. Now you have become the needle." At this the friend bowed again, said his farewells, and departed.

When looking at the fourth kata, Ippon Me Mae, you can see in Figures #*1* through #*4* the movement of the blade a little more clearly. The movement of the down stroke is a little different, going to the right side of the body instead of to the left. This is from the Mori-Ryu Iai-do, but the results are the same. It is a good idea to

Fig. 1

Fig. 2

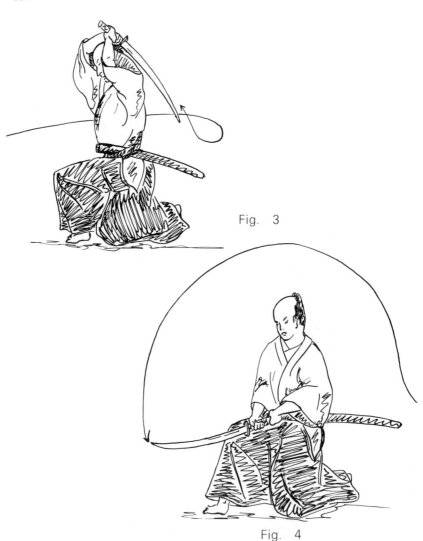

Fig. 3

Fig. 4

practice both sides, because sometimes space will not allow a left-sided finishing cut.

The next figures *5, 6, and 7* show a standing cut from a sitting position. This is done by rising straight up, bringing your right foot forward, and then aligning your left foot to your right. Next, take

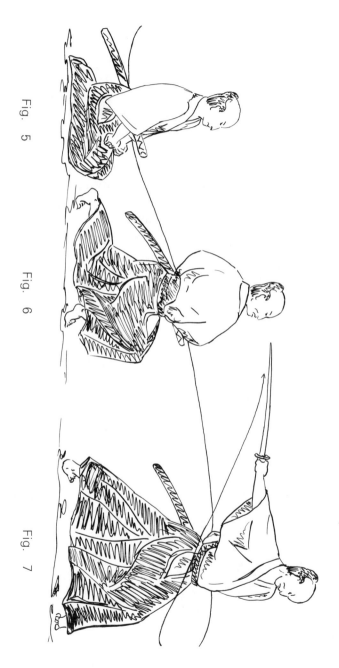

Fig. 5

Fig. 6

Fig. 7

126

hold of the handle and step out again with your right foot. If you will note the last figure #7, the right foot is positioned at a parallel angle with your body. The Bujutsu for this movement occurs when someone is standing over you and a few feet in front of you. You feel the intent of his attack and quickly rise, placing your right foot behind his front leg, squatting on your hips and putting pressure on his knee. This will cause him to fall backwards and allow you to make your cut successfully. Never take your eyes off of the opponent as you replace the sword into the saya. Step back with your right foot and resume the sitting position.

Figure #2 shows one way to perfect your timing and accuracy in Iai. You can start this exercise by having a friend toss up oranges or limes for you to use to make your cuts. Remember, go through each movement, and never leave out anything. The smallest movement is usually the most important. When you feel this is no longer a challenge, sit with your back to the thrower. Without a sound from

Fig. 8

either party, listen for the sound of the oranges leaving his hand and then turn and find your mark. I find sometimes when I practice alone, it is best to tie an apple on a string about head-high, letting the string swing back and forth. With my back to the apple, I turn and try to make the cut without cutting the string. When you get this down, try cutting the bottom of the apple and each time cutting only about $\frac{1}{4}$ of an inch at a time until only the stem is left. Another way to make the cut is to not let the apple swing; sit facing the apple and cut it in half on your first draw. Then on the second overhead cut, slice the apple again downward. It is important not to cut the string, but more important not to hit the apple with such force with the sword that you make it swing or break the stem. I must confess, however, with the prices of food these days, this can become expensive.

The least expensive way of practicing these cuts is to use a candle. Make yourself a small stand. I put four arms on my stand at different levels. Place a lighted candle on one of the arms and practice drawing and cutting off the flame. Do not cut the candle, just the wick so that the candle will go out. Do not knock the candle off of the stand. I once saw my master have such a stand with five candles, each candle was at a different level but all on a line going upward like a stairway. Sitting in the ready position very calmly, he rose to his feet making the draw. The next second there were only five small thin lines of smoke going to the ceiling. He held his sword in the air for a moment then replacing it in the saya he turned to me smiling and said, "I cannot train you in this way; I can only show you the way through these examples and watch you as you find your own path on the way."

Figures #9, 10, and 11 show an Iai movement from the Japanese film "Sanjuro" in which Toshiro Mifune is surrounded by attackers. The Iai movement starts with a left-handed draw to the rear for a cut, then passing the katana over the right hand he finishes cutting the other two with a downward circle leaving only one against one. He then went into Kenjutsu the Iai movement was finished with the second cut. These drawings help point out the difference between Iai Jutsu and Kenjutsu.

128

Fig. 9

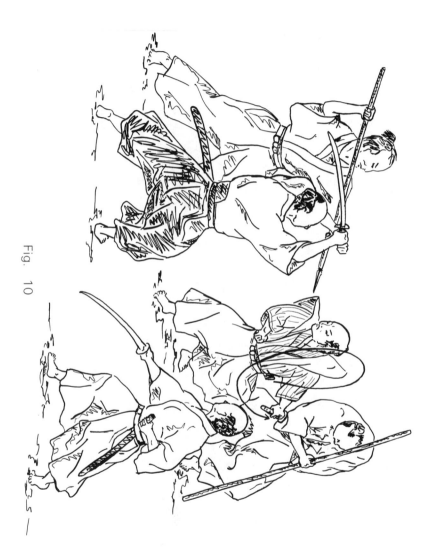

Fig. 10

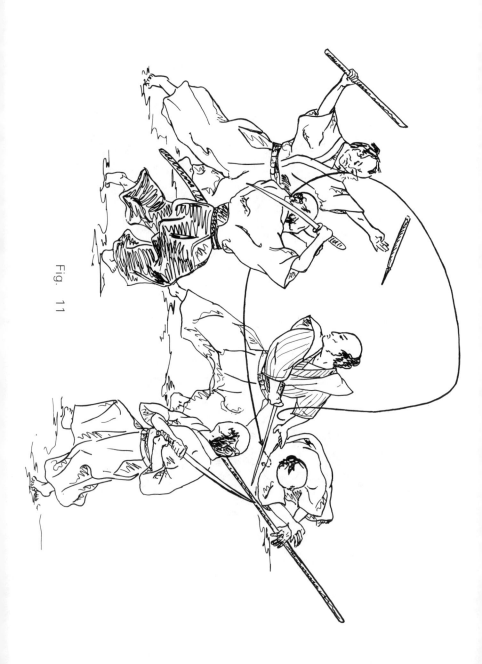

Fig. 11

CHAPTER NINE

Yato Uemoshichi Norikane   (Ronin of AKO)

Standing Iai Kata

Kata Number Five, Kesagiri
Kesagiri-Scapular Cut

In this kata, you cut the enemy's armpit and then, with a downward diagonal cut, cut the left shoulder. Please remember that the same sword etiquette applies when you are standing as when you are sitting. Keep your back straight, left wrist close to your waist, and eyes on your opponent at all times.

Since we have come this far and are preparing for the last of the Japan Kendo Federation Katas, I would like to relate another appropriate zen story:

One day I asked the Sword Master, "How can I cut with the sword if I do not do it?" "It cuts," he replied. "I have heard you say that several times before, so let me put it another way, how can I wait for the cut to happen if I am no longer there?" He replied that it waits at the highest tension. "And who or what is this (it)," I asked? "Once you have understood that, then you will have no further need for me. And if I tried to give you a clue at the cost of your own experience, then I would be the worst teacher and would deserve to be sacked! So let us stop talking about it and go on practicing," he concluded. Then one day, after a draw with the sword, the Master made a deep bow and broke off the lesson. "Just then IT cut!" he cried, as I stared at him bewildered. And when at last I understood what he meant, I could not suppress a sudden whoop of delight. "What I have said," the Master told me, surely was not praise, only a statement that ought not touch you. Nor was my sword meant for you, for you are entirely innocent of this cut. You remained this time absolutely without purpose in the highest tension, so that the cut fell from you like a ripe fruit. Now, go on practicing as if nothing had happened." "I am afraid I do not understand anything more at all." I answered, "even the simplest things have gotten in a muddle. Is it I who cuts with the sword, or is it the sword that draws me into the state of highest tension? Do I cut the goal or does the goal cut me? Is it spiritual when seen by the eyes of the spirit—or both or neither? Sword, goal, ego all melt into one another so that I can no longer separate them. And even the need to separate have gone. For as soon as I take the sword and cut, everything becomes so clear and straight-forward and so ridiculously simple." "Now at last," the Master broke in, "the sword edge has cut right through you."[1]

[1]Eugene Herrigel, *Zen in the Art of Archery* (Pantheon Books, N. Y.: 1953) Author's Note: The word sword has taken the place of the word archery.

Fig. 91   Fig. 92

Always keep in mind there is much more to Iai-do than meets the eye. Does the leaf leave the limb or does the limb leave the leaf? The point here is, do you control the drawing, or does the sword use you as a means of it's self-expression? Remember if you are having trouble with your Iai-do at this point stop. Go back and look at what you are doing. You may not be ready to continue yet. Do not be in a hurry to rush in deep water until you know how to swim: no one is drowning.

While you are moving forward in this first action, place your left hand on the saya and the right hand on the handle. Now turn the saya over so that the cutting edge is turned up. Push the sword guard forward with the thumb of your left hand. (See Figure #91.)

Stepping forward with the right leg, start the blade out of the saya. (See Figure #92.)

When the right foot has completed its forward step, the blade should have completed its cut. The cut is made diagonally upward

Fig. 93

and your sword hand should stop its upward movement when it is about 20° upward from your right shoulder. (See Figure #93.)

Now without moving your feet or body, take hold of the sword handle with your left hand. (See Figure #94.)

Without moving your leg position, deliver a downward cut to the enemy's left shoulder. The hands should stop even with your navel. The Ha of the blade should be turned about 15° outward and the kissaki downward. (See Figure #95.)

The next movement is to bring your katana to the Hassō position while bringing the right foot to the rear. The Hassō position with

Fig. 94   Fig. 95

136

the katana means that you are in waiting for the enemy's next move. The tsuba will be in line with your chin. (See Figure #96.) Note that the Hassō and right foot movements are done simultaneously.

Next, taking a step back with your left foot, place your left hand around the opening of the saya. Be sure that your wrist is against your waist. Now do chiburi (shaking the blood off of the blade). This is done by making an arc over your head and then bringing the blade downward. (See Figure #97 and #98.) Stop the blade's arc even with the angle of your right leg.

Fig. 96

Fig. 97

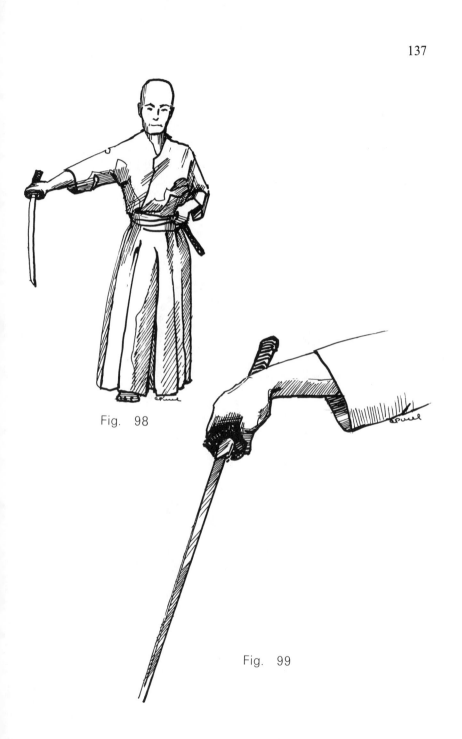

Fig. 98

Fig. 99

138

Figure #99 shows the wrist bent while doing chiburi, this is incorrect.

The last movement in this as in all katas is to replace the katana in the saya. Bring the rear foot to the front foot while you are making the return and assume the Taito Shisei position. (See Figure #100.) Note that the taito shisei position is not shown. See Kata Ukenagashi.

Fig. 100

CHAPTER TEN

Sugaya Hannojo Masatoshi

Morote-Suki

Two Hand Thrust
Kata Number Six

Before we get into the last two katas of this Ryu, I would like to point out again that Iai-do is made up of two very important parts: technique and spiritual training. I personally feel that the spiritual aspect of the art is even more important than the technical. You must enter into the enemy's attack to defeat him, through his psychological weaknesses.

This, what may be termed the "non-interfering" attitude of mind, constitutes the most vital element in the art of fencing as well as in Zen. If there is any room left even for the breadth of a hair between two actions, this is interruption. When the hands are clapped, the sound issues without a moments deliberation. The sound does not wait and think before it issues. There is no mediacy here, one movement follows another without being interrupted by one's conscious mind. If you are troubled and cogitate about what to do, seeing the opponent about to strike you down, you give him room, that is, a happy chance for his deadly blow. Let your defense follow the attack without a moment's interruption and there will be no two separate movements to be known as attack and defense. This immediateness of action on your part will inevitably end in the opponent's self-defeat. It is like a boat smoothly gliding down the rapids; in Zen, and in fencing as well, a mind of no-hesitation, no-interruptions, and no-mediacy, is highly valued.[1]

I sometimes feel that when the marionette master puts his mind wholly into the play, his state of mind attains something

[1] D. T. Suzuki, *Essays in Zen Buddhism*, Forward by Christmas Humphreys, (Samuel Weiser Inc.: N.Y, N.Y.) p. 363

of the swordman's. He is then not conscious of the distinction between himself and the doll he manipulates. The play becomes really an art when the master enters into a state of emptiness. Some may see a difference between the marionette master and the swordsman because the latter's confronting a living personality who is aiming every movement at striking you down. But my way of thinking is different, in as much as both have realized the state of identity, it must operate alike regardless of individual objectives.

When the identity is realized, I as a swordsman see no opponent confronting me and threatening to strike me. I seem to transfrom myself into the opponent, and every movement he makes as well as every thought he conceives are felt as if they were all my own and I intuitively, or rather unconsciously, know when and how to strike him. All seems to be so natural.[2]

Starting this kata, Morote-suki, you are attacked from the front and rear. You cut the temple and thrust the solar plexus of the enemy in front of you. Then turning 180° to the rear, you deliver a downstroke to the enemy to the rear. After delivering this second cut, you turn back and deliver a final cut to the front.

Turning the saya so the Ha is up, step out with your left foot and start your draw. (See Figure #101.)

Now, taking a second step with the right foot, finish the draw and cut the enemy's temple. (See Figure #102.)

Taking a chu-dan or center position with the sword (end of the handle at your navel and the point of the blade at the enemy's throat), place both hands on the handle and align the rear foot with the front. (See Figure #103.)

Moving the right foot forward, lower the tip of your sword to a level even with the enemy's solar plexus. (See Figure #104.) Note that you should stamp the right foot on the floor as you make this thrust.

As you center your left foot to the front foot, turn to the left

[2]Ibid pp. 205–204

Fig. 101

Fig. 102

Fig. 103

Fig. 104

raising the katana over your head. (See Figures #105 and #105A for rear views of this move.)

Now turn fully 180° to the rear and stepping out with the right foot and with the katana over the head, deliver a downward cut to the enemy's head. (See Figure #106.)

Now turning a full 180° back to the right, return to your starting position of the last move. The katana should be over your head as in Figure #106. You are now facing the first enemy. Deliver a downward cut to his head. Finish this movement as in Figure #107.

Without moving your feet, execute chi-buri to the right side of your body. (See Figure #108.) Remember that the left hand moves the saya back. All other chiburi movements are the same as in previous katas.

Fig. 105

Fig. 105A

Fig. 106

Fig. 107

Fig. 108

Sanpogiri

Kata Number Seven
Three-Directional Cut

This kata starts out with the same movements as Morote-suki except that instead of turning the saya completely so that the Ha of the blade is turned up, turn the saya only half way. The Ha is away from you. The action of this kata starts when you are faced with three enemies to the front, right and left sides. You will deliver three overhead cuts in succession: first the right, then the left, and lastly the final front cut.

Moving the left foot forward, take hold of the handle with both hands. Sensing the attack of the enemy on your right side, step with the right foot to the right drawing the blade with your right hand and make your cut on his right temple. (See Figure #109.)

Fig. 109

Without moving your feet, look to the left and , pivoting on the balls of your feet, take hold of the handle with both hands and raise the katana over your head. Then turn. (See Figure #*110.*)

Now deliver a downward cut to the enemy on your left. Stop the blade in the chu-dan. (See Figure #*111.*)

Raising the sword as in Figure #*112,* again turn to the front using the balls of the feet.

Then, stepping with the right foot, deliver the third downward cut. (See Figure #*113.*)

Stepping back with the right foot so the right foot is behind the left one, take the position with the katana called Morote go-dan (sword overhead indicating Zanshin Spiritual defense). (See Figure #*114.*)

Fig. 110

Fig. 111

Fig. 112

This position is usually held for a slow five count. Now step back with the left foot and place the left hand on the obi and saya. Then start your chiburi movement. (See Figure #*115*.) Be sure to arc the

Fig. 113

Fig. 114

katana from your center to the right side of your body.

When the chiburi action is complete, take hold of the opening of the saya with your left hand. The left foot should still be in the rear. Then start your return. When the return is complete, bring the left foot to the right. Thumb on the tsuba and assume taito-shisei standing. (See Figure #*116*.)

This completes the seven katas making up the Japan Kendo Federation Iai-do. Remember that when the sword is properly handled, it helps us in an efficient way to contribute to the cultivation of the mind and spirit.

Fig. 115   Fig. 116

CHAPTER ELEVEN

Okuda Magodayu Shigemori   (Ronin of AKO)

Bunki of Iai-do

The Inner Workings of Iai

Before we get into this chapter on the actual working movement of the art of Iai-do, I must explain something. Sometimes it is hard for the western mind to perceive that any martial art has a philosophy. But, please keep in mind that the very use of the word Iai-do and the wearing of the hakama with the Samurai sword are the marks of the adoption of the cultural heritage of the Japanese. All traditional arts from Japan are highly formalized and structural, often with rituals which to many outsiders may seem wasteful or superficial. To master any of these arts requires long years of training and most important, self-sacrifice.

Let your mind wander back to sixteenth-century Japan and read this story told by an old Zen master. This Master's name was Konto-Okuda. Now, Konto was said to be the greatest Iai-Jutsu master of Japan during his time. Many students of the art tried to test their skills against him but none is said to ever have succeeded in beating him. Most were beaten long before their hands ever touched their swords. Konto was a man of about fifty years, not excessively large, but about average in build. He kept his head shaved to the point that the skin almost shined. He seemed to have an air of humility about him but a close look into his eyes sent a chill down your back. The thing most distinctive about him were the two swords that he carried. The saya were not of the high gloss we would expect, but more like the color of black charcoal. The sword guards were a little larger than most and the handles were wrapped in black cord. They engendered a mysterious feeling as did the man himself. And yet, deep inside, you could not but feel a warmth of understanding in him.

One day as the sun was slowly declining behind the mountain and the chill of the evening was crawling upon the little monastery where Konto lived, a young man in his teens appeared at the outer gates. A Zen priest was lighting the gate lantern, when the young man asked, "Is this the monastery where Master Konto-Okuda resides?" Not stopping his duties, the priest pointed to a small door within the gates. The young boy bowed and started towards the door. Just as he was about to let his presence be known, the small door slid open. The young boy was startled for a moment, not knowing what to say. Then dropping to his knees the lad spoke, "Oh, please Master, you must teach me to be a master of Iai like yourself." The man in the door remained silent for a moment, which seemed like an eternity to the young man, but then as quickly as the door had opened, it shut. As he stayed in this kneeling position, the boy could not believe his ears; the Master had shut the door on him, Soto Mamoto, who had given up everything to seek out this Iai Master. Well, this just would not do; no one was going to shut a door in his face, master or not, without at least answering the question he had come so far to ask. Jumping to his feet, the young man quickly went up the two small steps and, knocking on the door, proclaimed in a loud voice, "You in there, who so rudely shut this door, I demand you come back out here and speak to me. I have but one question to ask you, and you will answer it before this night is through or my name is not Soto Mamoto."

The door slid open, as if by mysterious powers of its own. And there, out of nowhere, stood Konto-Okuda. As Soto looked into his eyes, he felt his knees starting to bend a little, and he knew it was not for the purpose of bowing. Looking deep into Soto's eyes, almost as if he were looking through him, not changing his facial expression or raising his voice, Konto said, "I hope your question is worthy of the answer." As Soto's head started to clear, he found himself on the ground in front of the small closed door. Lying there slowly moving his head from left to right, looking about, was convinced that he had been hit from behind. But to his suprise, he was all alone, with nothing but the flickering of the candle in the lantern at the front gate disturbing the stillness. He just could not believe it: one minute he was on the step and the next second on the ground. Now more than ever, Soto felt compelled to become the student of this man.

As the dampness of the evening dew crept into Soto's kimono there on the ground, it occurred to him to open the door and confront the Master. But as he started to rise, his head hurt terribly and the thought of opening the door vanished.

Taking up a kneeling position in front of the steps, Soto waited. "The Master has to come through the door sooner or later," Soto surmised, "and when he does he will see how humble I have made myself. He will have to accept me as a student then."

Minutes turned into hours, and the hours brought the cold mountain night. Slowly his eyes started to close, and he fell into a deep slumber. When he opened his eyes, he felt the warmth of the morning sun on his back. Quickly looking up at the door, he saw that it was still shut. "Good", he thought, "he has not left yet and when he does, I will be waiting." Morning turned into afternoon and his legs began to ache. His back felt as if trampled by oxen, and his throat was parched. "Why does not the Master come out?" he thought. "I do not know if I can stay here much longer." All at once there was an indescribable pain across his back. Again and again he felt a stick come crashing down upon him. As he tried to get to his feet to deflect the blows, he found his legs would not cooperate and he tumbled, falling flat upon his face. Then the blows changed from his back to his buttocks. He pulled with his arms using all the strength left in his body until he was under the steps and safe from the madman. Looking through the steps at his attacker he saw Konto-Okuda shouldering a long piece of bamboo and laughing to the heavens. Konto's voice roared with laughter, "Where is this man who demands to ask me but one question? Could that be him I see under my house, he who demanded last night, and now acts like a dog and hides beneath my dwelling?" Then as the words echoed, Konto went up the steps and Soto could hear the sliding of the door as it closed. Kneeling under the steps, trying to get the blood to circulate again in his legs, Soto could not help thinking to himself, "This man is stark raving mad, no wonder he is known as the greatest Iai-jutsu-ist. A person would have to be mad to deal with such a man." Just then he heard the door slide open above him, and a torrent of water came pouring down upon him. "There, demanding-one with no manners, let me try and clean your outside while you do something with that you call a brain."

That was enough. Out from under the steps Soto came. "Master" he shouted, "If you are not going to accept me as a student, then at least say so and I will be on my way." "Accept you?" Konto laughed, "You who came to me first demanding, then tried to show humility by kneeling all night outside my door, but was without humility enough to stay awake. Want you? No, I do not want you."

"So!" Soto broke in, "I will be on my way! Maybe I did start off on the wrong foot, and maybe I deserved the beating, but after all I have been through, don't you think you could at least answer my one question?"

Konto put his finger to the side of his nose and looked straight into Soto's face. For the first time Soto began to know fear. With a half-smile on his face but a frown upon his brow, Konto said almost in a whisper, "Tell me, little one, not that it really matters, what is your question?" Konto started down the steps, slowly placing his hand on the handle of his sword. "Come here so we can talk, little one." He was still moving forward towards Soto. Soto felt this was a dream, he could feel the Master getting close, but he did not seem to see his body moving, Konto reached out with his right hand and grabbed the boy by his hair. "Now demanding one," Konto exclaimed, holding him so that this face looked straight into the afternoon sun, "Tell me what is this most important question?" Soto felt his neck was about to break and he knew he was either about to die or have his question answered.

"What is this question, demanding one?" Konto said again softly, with eyes ablaze.

"Let go of my hair so I can stand up and I will tell you," Soto replied. Konto released his grip and it seemed to Soto like the hair on his head had grown a foot. Now Soto dropped to his knees at the Master's feet and without looking up started to explain his question.

"Master, as I have said, my name is Soto Mamoto and I come from Kyushu. My father was the fencing master at Kumamoto

Castle until he was killed by two ronin six months ago. It was at this time that I started on my journey to find you, Master." Konto broke in, "What was your father's name, little one?" "Shin No Fuji Mamoto," Soto replied. "Not Shin No Fuji Mamoto of Higo perfecture?" "Yes," Soto replied. Konto could scarely believe it. Shin No Fuji and he had grown up together, fought side by side in the castle wars, got drunk together many times and eventually fell in love with the same woman. But he had not heard from his good friend in many years. Quickly, Konto's mind snapped back to the boy. "Tell me, little one, what was your mother's name? And is she not worried about her son so far away at a time she might need him most?" he demanded.

"Master, her name was Shimoke-Kuto, but she died when I was born and I only know of her from my father's uncle. My father would never let her name be spoken in his presence."

Konto reached down and put his hand under the boy's chin, lifting it so he could study the story on his face. Indeed, Konto thought, this is Shimoko's child. She was the most beautiful woman he had ever known and through this little one she still lived.

Just then a loud voice from the monastery gate cut short Konto's memories. The voice was so loud that it startled Soto, and he jumped to his feet. Konto reached out and pushed the boy to one side behind him. Two men standing at the gate moved toward him. Konto placed his hands inside his kimono, and turned to face them, and spoke, "My name is Konto-Okuda. What do you seek here?" One of the men replied, "We do not wish to hurt you, old man, we have come for that one, there," and pointed at the little one.

"And what do you wish of him, may I ask?" questioned Konto. "That is none of your business," answered the ronin. "But you see it is my business, smelly one, for the one you seek is my student and therefore I am responsible for all of his actions," Konto retorted. The ronin laughed smugly, then turned back to Konto and said, "So bold one, who is acquainted with the Gods, you are responsible for this little one. Then I suggest that you make yourself ready to meet your responsiblities." Konto remained silent and let his body relax. He studied the ronin eyes, never changing his own expression nor removing his hands from under his kimono. As the ronin drew his katana, his swift hands became only a blur to Soto's eyes but more unbelievable to the boy was that the Master's entire body became a blur to the ronin movement. With the quickness of a mountain cat, the ronin tried to block what his eyes could not truly see. But it was too late, for when the ronin finally realized that the sword was coming from the old man's saya, he had already felt the Ha cutting deep into his flesh. The ronin tumbled dead at Konto's feet. Konto quickly turned to face the other ronin, but he had vanished as suddenly as the life which Konto had just taken. Now making a circle over his head with his katana and a snapping movement with his wrist, he removed the blood from the end of his sword. Before Soto's mind had digested this movement, the sword was back in its resting place. Soto's heart was pounding like the sound of an attack drum and finally realizing that it was over, he ran to Konto's side. Looking down at the dead ronin and then to the Master, he began to weep. "Master, these were the Samurai who killed my father! As my father was dying, he told me of you, he said to come here and to become your student."

"Not now, little one," Konto interrupted, "We will have plenty of time later to talk about such things. We must take care of first things first. This lifeless body must be cared for and we must pray for his misguided soul. Now go to my room and try to rest while I take care of these matters."

It was late evening when Soto heard the Master come in. He did not move from where he had been sleeping, but just lay there thinking never before had he known such a man, such a great warrior, and he knew that the answer to his question was within reach.

When Soto awoke the next morning he could see the Master making tea. Quickly going over to where Konto was, he knelt down and, taking the kettle from the fire, began to pour the master's tea. "If I am going to be your student, master, you must allow me to do my duties. A student does not sleep while his Master makes tea."

"It is good you know such things," Konto smiled. As they sipped their tea and warmed their bodies by the fire, Konto broke the silence and said, "Well, little one, I feel it is time we had our talk. You have come all this way to ask a question, but I must warn you that some questions are better never asked, for once you ask and seek the answer, you will be drawn into the trap of life. The answer could lure you away from all things that now seem important. You may start on the endless circle I have travelled, and find only that the end is no end at all. The revenge you hold in your heart for this other man may only bear bitter fruit, that neither you nor anyone else will ever be able to digest. With these things in mind, you may ask your question."

Soto looked at the Master for a minute reflectively, put his cup down and began to speak. "Master, before my father died he made me promise to revenge his death. But in a way, I do not understand. He said I would only be able to set his spirit at rest by finding the answer to the sound of one hand clapping. He said unless I truly find this answer, the ronin would surely kill me and my death would be of no purpose. He then told me of you and explained if there was anyone on earth who could help me with the problem it would be you."

Konto, looking into his tea cup, could not help but smile to himself, for he knew now without a doubt what he had suspicioned all along. Shin No Fuji had sent the little one on an endless journey for his own safety. He knew Soto would never leave the monastery now until he had found the answer. The answer would take many years. By the time he knew the answer, he would have forgotten why it was so important in the first place.

Soto cleared his throat, and the Master looked up. The boy continued, "Master, do you know the answer?"

"Oh yes, I know the answer, little one! But first let me ask you a question. Do you know the sound of two hands clapping?"

"Is it important to know the sound of two hands, Master?" Soto replied. Konto poured himself a little more tea. "Yes, I am afraid so, little one, before you get into the water, you must first learn to swim. Remember if you are going to be my student and search for the answer of one hand, I can only instruct you in the use of the sword, I cannot teach you, you must teach yourself. The sound of two hands clapping is one of the most vital elements in the art of kenjutsu, as well as in Zen. Always remember, little one, when the hands are clapped, the sound is heard without a moment's deliberation. If there is any room left even for a breath of air between these two actions, there is interruption. The sound does not wait and think before it issues, one movement follows another without being interrupted by one's conscious mind. Do you understand this, little one?"

"I must confess, master, I do not think I do," Soto replied. "Well, do not worry about it now," Konto smiled, "we have plenty of time and you must start your duties before the morning wastes away."

Bunkai

In truly learning the Bunkai of swordmanship, you must find your circle and know the enemy's circle. When you have done this let him enter your circle. You then must advance into his until you have become intertwined with his attack. Now there is not attack and counter, only attack. This movement in Zen is called:

Seizing the enemy's spear and using it as the weapon to kill him.[1]

Explaining this is very difficult, but in his movement of attack, for one second you become the attacker. If you think of defending yourself you will surely feel the cut of his sword, but if you rush forward under his attack, pressing your own attack, he will slowly be defeated. Remember there are only eight directions of attack and eight directions of defense. The diagrams illustrate this:

Figure #1 has started his attack
Plate B
Figure #2 has submerged into Figure #1 attack leaving no attack or defense.

[1]Ibid pp. 96

Figure #1 (A)

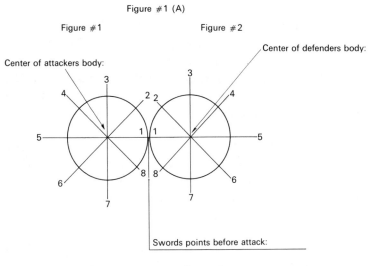

Figure #1   Figure #2

Center of defenders body:

Center of attackers body:

Swords points before attack:

Figure #1   Figure #2

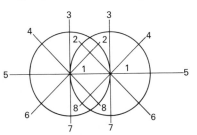

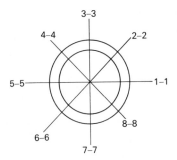

Figures #1 and #2 submerged:

Bunki of Iai-do

Starting with Ukenagashi kata, the three illustrations will explain the actual movement of this kata or the bunki. In the bunki we are only interested in the three defending movements.

1.   Figure #*117*: The enemy is sitting to your left and attacks you. Drawing your katana as the enemy steps with his left foot to make his attack, you turn your body just a little toward the attacker and block.

2.   Figure #*118*: Rise to your feet, holding your katana in the previous blocking manner so that the enemy's sword slides down it and puts him off balance. Note: Do not forget to shift your feet. Refer to page #*128* for further instructions.

3.   Figure #*119*: Drawing the left foot back, make your cut to the enemy's left shoulder.

Note that returning the blade to the saya is not part of the bunki. This is part of the kata. For further information refer to the Ukenagashi Kata.

Fig.   117

Fig. 118

Fig. 119

Bunki

Iai-Do-Hiza Kata-Tsuka-Ate has four movements, but I feel that the last strike is not Iai, but should be regarded as a seperate sword cut. Therefore at my discretion I am only showing the first three movements as bunki.

1. Figure #120: The enemy in front attacks. Rise to meet the attack on your right foot and strike the attacker in the solar plexus with the butt of your katana handle.

2. Figure #121 shows that the first enemy has fallen, but you are now attacked from behind. Quickly pull the saya from the katana, which is done by moving your left hand back to your waist and leaving your right arm extended.

3. Figure #122 shows you turning your upper body towards the attacker and thrusting into the enemy's solar plexus with the tip of your sword. To finish as in the kata, you would place the katana overhead and deliver a killing blow to the first attacker. Then you are again facing front and should slide one step forward with your right foot. For the katana's return, see Tsuka-ata Kata.

Fig. 120

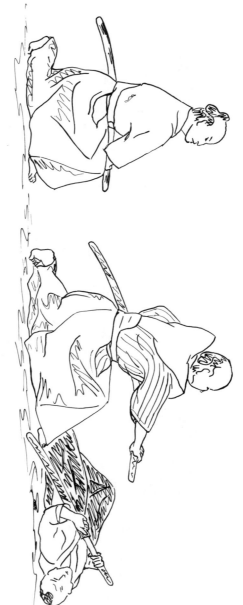

Fig. 121

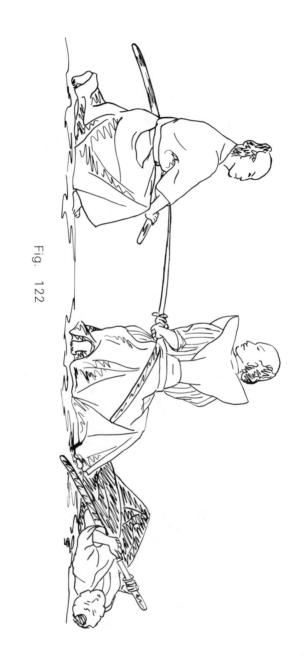

Fig. 122

Bunki

Tachi-Iai-Do Kesagiri bunki has four movements.

1. While you are walking, the enemy attacks you from the front. With your right foot forward, turn the cutting edge of your katana up and start your draw. (See Figure #123.)

Figure #124 shows the blade on its way. It is well to note here that if you study this drawing carefully you will note you are to be directly under the enemy's blade.

2. Now the blade has made contact with the enemy's right armpit. This cut must continue until your hand is even with the enemy's right shoulder. (See Figure #125.)

3. Take hold of the handle of your katana with your left hand and raise it to the right and above your head. (See Figure 126.)

4. Without delay, deliver your final cut through the enemy's left shoulder. This should separate the top of his body from the

Fig. 123

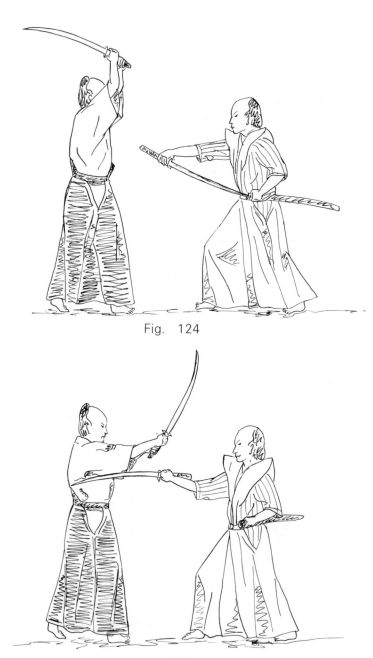

Fig. 124

Fig. 125

bottom. (See Figure #127.) To make the return, refer to Kesagiri kata.

Fig. 126

Fig. 127

Morote-suki Kata (Double-handed thrust)

This kata includes two attackers, one in front and one in back. Taking one step with your left foot, place your hand on the handle of your sword. Now, taking a step with your right foot, draw your katana and cut the enemy with a Yoko (Side) Men. (See Figure *#128.*)

Now taking a chu-dan (center position), bring the rear foot to the front. (See Figure *#129.*)

Now stepping out with the right foot and stamping it on the floor, make a double-handed thrust to the enemy's solar plexus. (See Figure *#130.*)

Fig. 128

Bring the rear foot about eighteen inches over to your left, pivot to the rear and raise the katana over your head. (See Figure #131.)

Your left foot should be forward. Next step with your right foot forward and deliver a downward cut to the enemy in the rear.

Pivoting on the balls of your feet, turn to the right 180° and raise the katana over your head. Step forward with your right foot and make your final downward cut to the first attacker. (See Figure #132.) Then, staying in the same position, execute chiburi.

Fig. 129

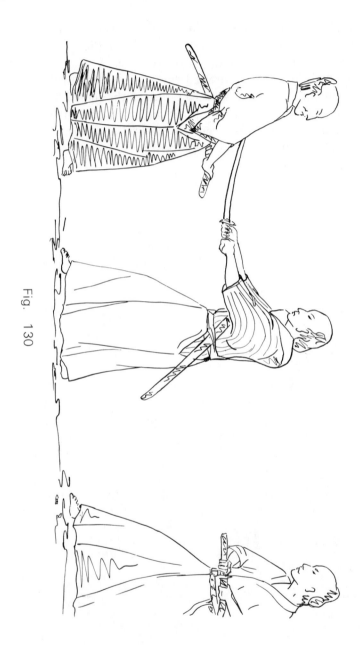

Fig. 130

Fig. 131

Fig. 132

CHAPTER TWELVE

Nakamura Kansuke Masatoki   (Ronin of AKO)

Sword Testing

When I think of testing the Japanese sword, I recall the legend of the great swordsmith, Okazaki Masamune. Masamune's swords are held in the greatest admiration by all sword collectors for their outstanding quality. The Muramasa sword made by one of his students was by no means something of lesser quality, but the master is said to have something divine in his sword that no other maker has ever been able to duplicate. The legend goes as follows: When someone was trying to test the sharpness of a Muramasa, he placed it in a current of water and watched how it acted against the dead leaves flowing down-stream. He saw that every leaf that met the blade was cut in twain. He then placed a Masamune, and he was surprised to find that the leaves avoided the blade. The Masamune was not bent on killing, it was more than a cutting implement, where as the Muramasa could not go beyond cutting, there was nothing divinely inspiring in it.[1]

At the same time you must keep in mind this is only a Japanese legend and that even swords made by the same maker were made one at a time. Each sword was forged individually allowing possibilities for errors and, in some cases, flaws. These errors and flaws sometimes only show up in testing the blade. I am sure the swordsmith had many tests that he, or his assistants, conducted before the product of his unique craftmanship was handed over to its prospective buyer. Testing a sword made for the purpose of defending ones life in battle at times meant cutting through heavy pieces of armor worn by the bushi. Therefore, most bushi would not accept a sword without subjecting it to a series of cutting tests that he or another Samurai who specialized in testing swords would perform. If the sword did not meet the highest of standards, it was discarded or melted down to make a spear or halberd. The Samurai who tested swords was licensed or appointed by the Shogun to

[1]Ibid pp 92

execute condemned criminals. This allowed the use of live bodies for testing. The event was held with strict ceremonial formality. Witnesses were selected, special clothing was worn, and most importantly, upon conclusion all was recorded and a certificate was issued to certify the testing results. The sword tester then signed the nakago or tang of the sword in gold, giving the date, place, and whatever cut that he used against the victim and how many cuts were made.

There were, in addition, tests that did not require live bodies. But, before exploring that, I would like to explain the testing procedure from the beginning.

When a sword was to be tested, it had to be prepared by making a special handle for it. (See Figure #133,)

Fig. 133

This handle was made from two pieces of hard wood with adjustable holes (mekugi). The two metal bands around the handle slide up and down to assure a tight fit. Most professional testers carried their own testing handle which was made with his specific specifications.

There is much difference between doing Iai-do and actually cutting something. As I have stated, it is almost impossible to learn Iai-do to its fullest without knowing Kendo. Kendo teaches you the proper hand positioning along with the most vital cutting movements of the wrist action.

Proper Hand Position

The hand position shown in Figure #134 is as follows:

1. Place the left hand on the handle so that the little finger is at the base of the kashira.

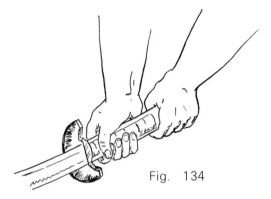

Fig. 134

2. Let the fingers wrap around the handle so that the top of the kashira is about even with the back side of your wrist; place your index finger on the kashira.

Note that the fourth finger is not wrapped around the handle. It balances the handle at the first joint from the end of the finger.

3. Now, place the right hand as shown in the diagram with the finger on the menuki.

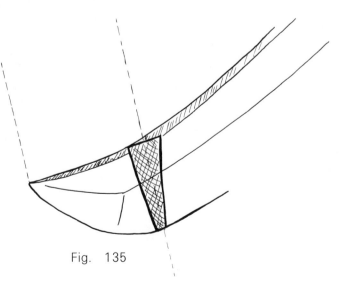

Fig. 135

4.   Raise the sword over your head and make a downward cut, stopping the kashira even with your navel. The hands must twist around the handle while executing this movement as if wringing a wet towel.

The next Figure #135 shows the actual part of the blade that you cut with.

This reinforced part of the blade is called the yokote. All cuts with a katana must be made with the first six to seven inches of the blade.

Figures #136 and #137 show the actual test cutting.

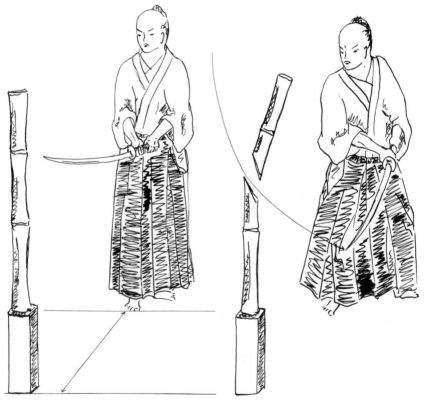

Fig.   136

The setup can be accomplished by getting a piece of bamboo three to four inches in diameter, and a square or round pole about four feet in length and seven to eight inches in diameter. Bury the pole upright in the ground about half way. You can either drill out a hole in the top of the pole so that the bamboo will slide inside or you can drive a dowel into the top of the pole so that about one-half foot protrudes from the top. Now, place the bamboo over this dowel. You may even have to tie it to the dowel. When you have secured the bamboo and are ready to make the cut, you must keep these things in mind:

1. Find the proper distance between you and the bamboo so that you will cut with only the first six to seven inches of the katana.
2. Decide which cut you will use. The heaven to earth cut shown in the diagram will be the easiest to start with.

Fig. 137

3. Make sure that your stance is correct. If you are cutting from right to left as in the drawing, your left foot is in the rear.
Note: This is very important because of the chance of an accident. If the cut is not clean, the blade may ricochet and cut your left leg. Remember to always keep the left leg in the rear.
4. Once you start your cut, it is absolutely necessary for you to follow all the way through. This will help to prevent a mishap due to a ricochet.
5. Be sure to cut the bamboo at an angle. If you try to cut straight across, you might chip the ha or, more probably, just break the bamboo.
6. The most important thing of all is to take this seriously.Make sure that you know what you are doing before you try it.

Another cutting test that is exciting is to cut through straw. After a straw bundle is prepared properly, it gives much the same feel as cutting the human body. This type of sword testing became popular after the Meiji prohibition of wearing the swords late in the eighteen-seventies. (See Figure #138.) The cut in the drawing would be the same as cutting through four bodies with one stroke. To prepare the straw for this test is fairly simple:

1. Select straw about four feet in length.
2. Select a green piece of bamboo about an inch and a half in diameter and two to three inches longer than the straw.
3. Roll the straw around the bamboo pole until you have a roll about one foot in diameter. Tie the ends and middle with a piece of cord.
4. Take the bundle and soak it in a bucket of water. I find a large garbage can best suited for this purpose. The bundle must stay submerged in the water until the straw is completely soaked through, generally twenty-four hours.
5. Now, remove the bundle and using a high test cord (not rope or twine), wrap the bundle as tightly as possible so that the bundle is about nine inches in diameter.
6. Place the bundle in the sun until it is dry. This usually takes about a day and a half.

When the straw is completely dry, it is ready for cutting.

Fig. 138

Place the bundle on a wooden block as in Figure #140, tie the ends down, and you are ready to make your test.

If you do not wish to prepare a block of wood like that in the drawing, I find a wooden pine stool very suitable. Get a stool three-and-a-half to four feet high with no back or armrests.

Place the bundle in the middle of the seat and tie the ends down to the supporting leg rungs. This cut involves only an overhead strike, as follows:

1. Determine your proper distance as in the previous test.
2. Place your feet apart, about two feet wider than your shoulders.
3. When you bring the katana down to make this cut, you must bend your knees slightly and push your ki down below your navel. Although this test seems fairly simple, I warn you that you will find it more difficult than you imagine.
4. Again, you must follow through mentally as well as physically to be successful.

Figure #139 shows a sword test using a piece of metal. I would not recommend this because you might destroy your katana.

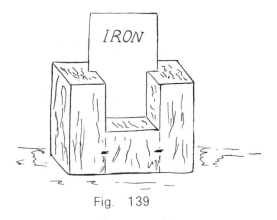

Fig. 139

Human Body Testing

Figure #*140* was the arrangement used for human bodies. The body was laid on a pile of sand, face up so that the back was stretched tight. The cuts were made diagonally.

Human testing was as often as not the case in medieval Japan. Figures #*141* through #*144* show different ways that these tests were performed. Many times after the initial cut, the pieces were stacked up and cut again and again until there was not a piece of human flesh left larger than a hand.

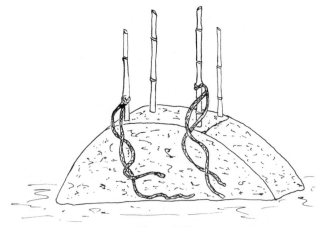

Fig. 140

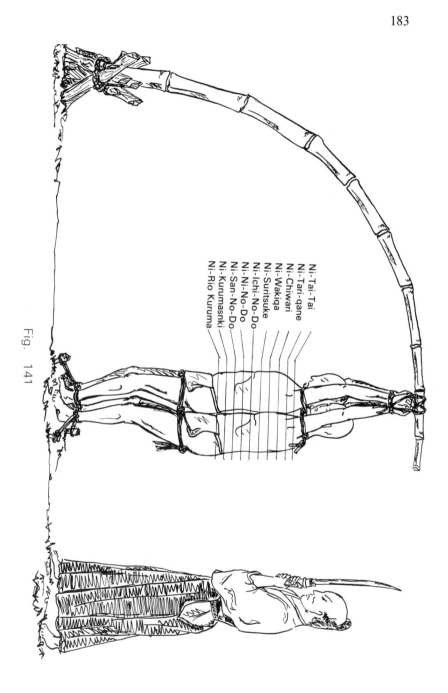

Ni-Tai-Tai
Ni-Tari-qane
Ni-Chiwari
Ni-Wakiqa
Ni-Suritsuke
Ni-Ichi-No-Do.
Ni-Ni-No-Do.
Ni-San-No-Do.
Ni-Kurumasnki
Ni-Rio Kuruma

Fig. 141

184

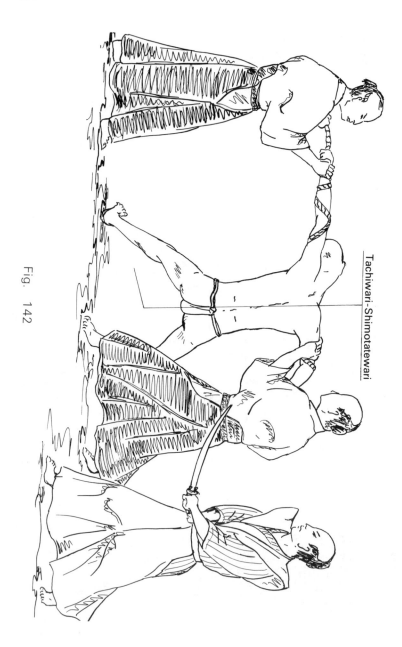

Fig. 142

Tachiwari-Shimotatewari

Two body Testing

Fig. 143

Ni-Rio Kuruma

Fig. 144

The last Figure #*145* shows many of the test cuts and their names. Starting with A and going through S, they are:

A. Kogesa
B. Okesa
C. Tachiwari
D. Tategesa
E. Sodesuri

187

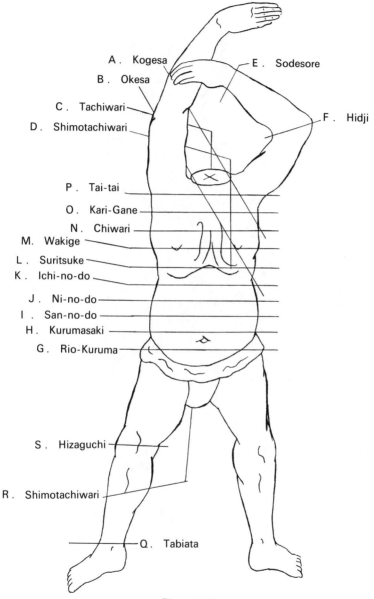

A . Kogesa
B . Okesa
C . Tachiwari
D . Shimotachiwari

E . Sodesore

F . Hidji

P . Tai-tai
O . Kari-Gane
N . Chiwari
M. Wakige
L . Suritsuke
K . Ichi-no-do
J . Ni-no-do
I . San-no-do
H . Kurumasaki
G . Rio-Kuruma

S . Hizaguchi

R . Shimotachiwari

Q . Tabiata

Fig. 145

CHAPTER THIRTEEN

Hayami Tozaemon Mitsutaka   (Ronin of AKO)

Mu Gai Ryu Hyo-do

Mu Gai Ryu Hyo-do is one of the older styles of Iai-Jutsu. I have been told by my Master, Mr. Shiyogo Kuniba, a student in the art, that there are only two or three schools left in all of Japan that teach this particular style. Considering the style, I feel the only reason it has a "do" instead of a "jujitsu," is because of the era. Swords are no longer used for fighting so to keep up with the modern age, we must change to the way it used to be. If we translate Mu Gai Ryu Hyo Do, another question comes up. Does the "do" in the name actually mean a way like Kendo or has it always been a way? Translated, the name means "Empty self style or drawing of the leopard's way." It seems that no one is really certain just how the style's name came about. Master Kuniba's father handed it down to him when he was just a young boy. The style had been known to only a small clan of bushi in the southern part of Japan around Shimonoseki.

Some of the outstanding charateristics of the style are:

1. Drawing starts when seated on your heels, with the balls of your feet on the floor instead of your insteps.
2. Every return of the blade ends with you in the Sonkyo position and then going to Tachi.
3. Instead of the back of the blade coming in front of your body as in the Japanese Kendo Federation style, in Mu Gai Ryu Hyo Do, it comes from the side of the shoulder in a horizontal position.
4. The most outstanding difference between this style and any other is the fact that you change the position of your feet with each cut. Some have said that this makes the style slower when delivering the second cut. To this I have no comment for I am but a student in the art and not a Master. Nevertheless, this extra movement does make you combine sword and body, so I feel that it has merit.

The complete style has twenty-four katas, twelve sitting and twelve standing. There are also twelve tsuka wazas and several saya wazas. It would be too involved to introduce you to all these at this time, so I have picked the katas and wazas that I feel would be appropriate at a beginner's level. These will consist of seiza kata, one tachi kata, several tsuka wazas and one saya waza. You will notice that I have chosen to use the bunki to illustrate Mu Gai Ryu Iai Hyo Do. I feel that this will help you to understand the movements more clearly.

You must keep in mind when practicing this ryu that it was practiced in Japan when Iai was a true way of life and will help you obtain an insight through intensive training within the old ryū-ha where the true spirit of the art is fully manifested.

Mu-Gai Ryu-Hyo Do

Za-Iai-Seiza Katas

1.	You	Useful
2.	Shin	Truce
3.	Tsuka-waza	Handle Technique
4.	Yoko Tsuka Tomoe	Side Handle Circle
5.	Te-Saya Waza	Hand Saya Technique
6.	Muchi-no-kimo-shippo	Lashing Tail
7.	Ten Te	Heaven Hand

Other Mu-Gai Ryu-Hyo-Do Katas I have not included in this printing:

1.	Ren	Training
2.	Sa	Difference
3.	Hibiki	Sound
4.	Hibiki Kaeshi	Sound Return
5.	Go	Friendship
6.	Zen-Go-Sen	Forward Backward Offense
7.	Ma-Ko-(Ma-Tsu-Ko)	Right in front
8.	Karatake	Empty

Kata Number One
You-Seiza
Useful-Sitting

1. As you feel the intent of the enemy's attack, look into his eyes.
   Sit on your heels with the balls of the feet on the floor. Do not
   move, but stay as relaxed as possible. Keep your hands on your
   thighs. (See Figure #1.)

Fig. 1

Fig. 2

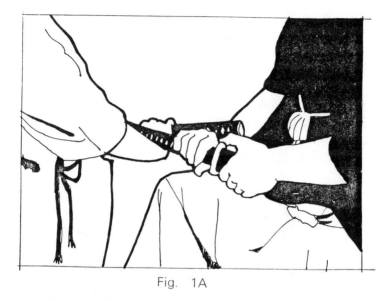

Fig. 1A

2. Let the enemy start his attack. Rise on your knees using your thigh muscles. Now, take hold of your katana, bring your right leg forward, and block the enemy's draw with the tsuka of your katana. (See Figure #2.)

Note: Figure #1A shows a close-up of this movement of

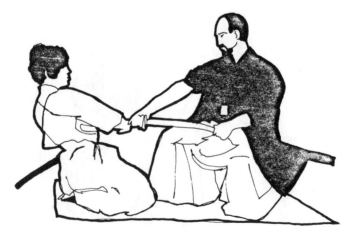

Fig.   3

pushing downward with the tsuka on the enemy' wrist preventing him from completing his draw. Please notice that the thumb is on the tsuba.

Push forward now with your katana keeping a downward pressure on the enemy's wrist forcing him down and backward. (See Figure #3.)

3. The katana has now cleared the saya and as you position it

Fig. 4

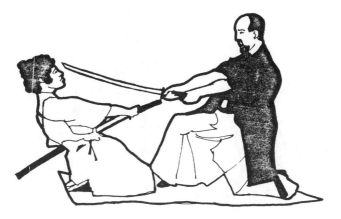

Fig. 5

over your head, the enemy again starts his attack. (See Figure
#4.)

4. Sliding forward about one-half foot with the right (forward)
    leg deliver a downward cut, cutting the head, solar plexus, and
    the right wrist. (See Figure #5.)

Fig.   6

Fig.   7

5. Chiburi: Bring the right leg back, step out with the left leg and make a circle over your head with the katana. Note that these two actions are done simultaneously. The shaking of the blood from the katana is like that of the Japan Kendo Federation's Iai-do Kata Number One except that you do not stand up. Stop the blade at a 45° angle. (See Figure #6.)

6. To replace the katana in the saya, place your left hand around the opening of the saya extending your thumb and index finger. Bring the back of the katana just below the tsuba between them. The tip of the blade will be pointing up and slightly over your left shoulder. (See Figure #7.)

7. As you slide the katana down through your thumb and index finger, push your right hand outward. Slide the front foot back to the rear foot, immobilize the waist and keep the right knee on the floor. The tip of your blade should now be at the opening. Note that these two actions must move as one: blade and front foot move together. Starting the katana in the saya so that it rides on its back, cutting side up, take the sonkyo position on the balls of the feet with the right knee on the floor. Your legs will be a 90° angle, your back straight, and your eyes

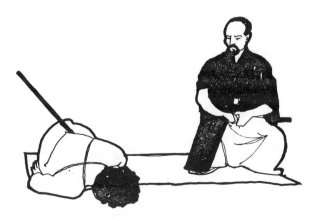

Fig. 8

looking at the attacker. As the blade comes to a stop, place your thumb on the tsuba and sit firmly on the balls of your feet. (See Figure #8.)

8. Tachi: Bring the left knee forward with the right knee remaining on the floor. Take your hands off of the katana and saya and place them on your thighs. Hold this position for about a three count. Now, replace your left hand on the saya with the thumb on the tsuba. Take your right hand and place it on the Kashira. Then slide your left foot forward and rise to your feet. Your left foot will be forward. Next, bring back your left foot to the right foot and align them. Assume Tachi. Note that the Tsuba will be positioned at your navel. Keep the sword in a horizontal position.

Prepare for the next action.

Kata Number Two
Shin-Seiza
Truce in Sitting

1. While sitting on your heels with the balls of the feet on the floor, knees about one and a half feet apart, back straight, head erect and looking straight into the opponent's eyes, you sense his intent to attack you.

Fig. 9

2. Placing your left hand on the saya, turn the saya so that the blade is pointing down. Place your thumb on the tsuba and push so that the habaki is exposed. (See Figure #9.)
3. Now the attacker makes his actions clear. You push the tsuka across your body to the right and take hold of it, but do not expose your wrist. (See Figure #10.)
4. Make your draw, moving your right foot forward, stamping it on the floor. Remember that you do not lean forward and that

Fig. 10

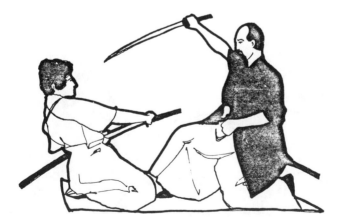

Fig. 11

you use your thigh muscles to rise straight up. Next, move your right foot. The finish of the draw and the stamping of the foot must come at the same time. The draw stops with the wrist even with the top of your head. Note that the attacker counters by returning to Seiza and reclining. (See Figure *#11*.)

5. Now, place the katana over your head as in Figure *#12*. Note that the attacker has lost his balance and has started to fall backwards.

Fig. 12

Fig. 13

6. Starting your downward cut, change feet and bring the right leg back and advance the left. As the downward cut is completed, the attacker's wrist falls off. (See Figure #13.) Note that you will advance forward about one foot with the changing of the legs. The balls of the feet are on the floor. The chiburi and sword return are the same as the previous kata.

Kata Number Three
Tsuka Waza
Handle technique

This is just one of the many tsuka wazas in Mu Gai Ryu IAI Hyo Do. I have included it for the sole purpose of letting the reader see the versatility of the style.

1. Sitting side by side with the attacker on your right, the attacker starts his draw. You rise straight up using your thigh muscles. (See Figure #14.)

Next, you step out with the left foot slightly forward toward the attacker. Place your hands on your katana and start to make your draw.

2. Instead of drawing the blade all the way out of the saya, stop about half way, placing the tsuka on the attacker's tsuka,

Fig. 14

Fig. 15

forcing him to return to Seiza. (See Figure #15.)

Note that Figure #14A shows a close-up of this movement. After you have stopped their attack, return to Seiza.

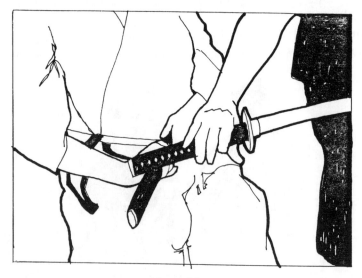

Fig. 14A

Kata Number Four
Yoko-Tsuka-Tomoe
Side handle circle

1. The attacker has caught you unaware and has advanced his attack before you can counter with a draw of your own. (See Figure #16.)
2. As the attacker takes advantage of his surprise, you fall backwards and to the right, using your right hand to catch your balance. Placing the left hand on your saya, thumb on the tsuba, pull the saya forward about two feet. (See Figure #17.)
3. The attacker now feels he has the full advantage of his attack for a "men" or head cut. You have now pulled the saya far enough out that the tsuba is even with your chin. (See Figure #18.)
4. As the attacker makes his downward cut, you block it using the tsuka of your katana. (See Figure #19.)
5. When the enemy's blade makes contact with your tsuka, start coming to the seiza position, keeping tension on his blade.

Fig. 16

Make a small circle to your left, holding his blade down enabling him to withdraw his katana. (See Figure #20.)

Fig. 17

Fig. 18

Fig. 19

Fig. 20

6. You have now resumed your seiza position. Move your right leg forward and pull the saya, attacking the enemy just under the chin with the tsukagashira of your katana. Note that your right knee will be in front and centered with the attacker's body. Keep your back straight and lock your elbows with the strike, then relax. (See Figure *#21*.)

Fig. 21

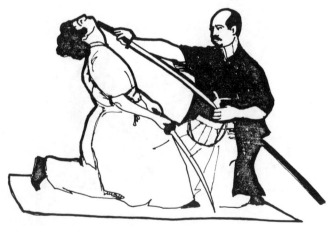

Fig. 22

7. Keeping your attack flowing, leave the right hand extended and pull the saya from the blade. The saya will return to the obi so that it will maintain its original position. (See Figure #22.)

8. As you withdraw the attack at the enemy's chin he changes his leg position and tries to counter. You quickly raise your katana over your head. Also change the position of your feet and slide about twelve inches forward. The left leg is now

Fig. 23

Fig. 24

forward and the back of the blade is resting between the thumb and index finger over the head. (See Figure #23.)

9. Using your left hand to guide and apply extensive pressure, bring your katana down in a circle in front of you, striking the enemy. (See Figure #24.)

10. Stop your attack when the tsuba is even with your waist and the kissaki of your katana is at the attacker's waist. (See Figure #25.)

11. Execute chiburi as in the previous katas.

12. Execute kaeshi (return of katana to saya) the same as in the previous katas.

13. Execute tachi the same as in the previous katas.

Fig. 25

Kata Number Five
Te-Saya-Waza
Hand sabert technique

1. Sitting beside you, the enemy starts his attack. Quickly reach over with your right hand and pull upwards on his saya. Your left hand simultaneously goes to your saya, thumb on the tsuba. (See Figure #26.)

2. While still pulling upward with your right hand, pivot on your left knee and bring your right leg forward. (See Figure #27.)
3. Your attacker has now lost his balance. Continue your own attack by taking hold of your own katana and trying to strike him in the face with the tsukagashira. (See Figure #28.)
4. The enemy has fallen back still further avoiding your tsukagashira attack. Now, bring your right leg back and step forward, gaining about one foot with your left leg. Deliver an

Fig. 26

Fig. 27

overheaded downward cut to the attacker's neck. (See Figure #29.)

5. Chiburi, kaishi, and tachi are repeated as in previous katas.

Fig. 28

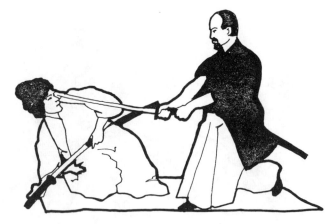

Fig. 29

Kata Number Six
Muchi-No-Kimo-Shippo
The Lashing Tail

It might be well to note here that this kata might have been the origin of the style's name. I must admit that when I have shown this particular kata to others in the art of Iai, they are somewhat surprised. I do not mean to imply they have not seen it before, but I feel they are surprised that a westerner would know about it.

1. The enemy attacks with sword already drawn. You quickly turn your saya with your left hand so that the cutting edge is pointing downward and take hold of the tsuka with your right hand. (See Figure *#30.*)

2. Pivoting on your right knee and bringing your left leg to a 90° angle to your right will move you across and in front of the attacker. This action allows your saya to connect with the

Fig. 30

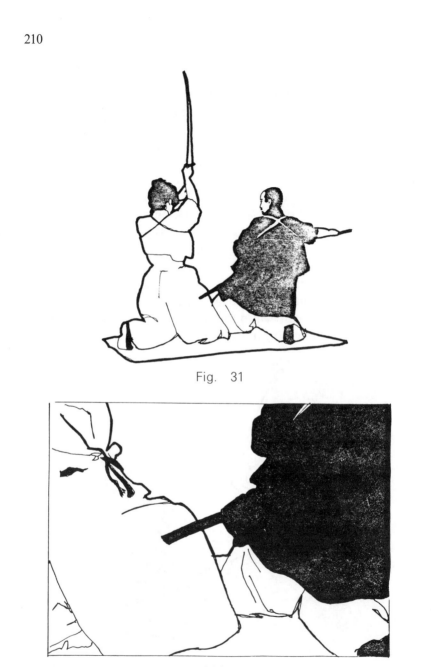

Fig. 31

Fig. 31A

attacker's leading knee and turn his body to the left and off balance. Note that as you are pivoting, you should pull the katana from the saya so that the back of the blade is towards you. (See Figure #31.)

Figure #31A is a close look at the saya position. The saya must hit the attacker in the bend of the knee and even with the knee cap.

3. While the enemy is trying to regain his balance and counter your attack, thrust into his solar plexus with the tip of your katana. The blade is perpendicular to the floor. You do not move the lower part of your body, but pivot from the waist up for the thrust. (See Figure #32.)

4. The attacker has now fallen backwards with the thrust. Moving the left leg back to your left, placing the katana over your

Fig.   32

head and sliding forward using your left foot, deliver a downward stroke to the enemy's left wrist. (See Figure #33.)

5. Chiburi, kaeshi, and tachi are repeated as in the previous katas.

Fig. 33

Kata Number Seven
Saya-Ushiro
Behind

1. When you are attacked from behind while in the seiza position, listen for the katana coming from the saya and the rustle of cloth as the enemy makes his attack. (See Figure #34.)

Fig. 34

2. Stepping forward with your right foot, take hold of your katana with your right hand. Place the left hand on the saya and turn the edge of the blade upwards. Pull the katana straight forward and upward. The tsukagashira is pointing upward and the kissaki towards the floor. The katana is still on your left side with the right arm across your body and forward. See Figure #35 which shows the beginning of this movement.

3. Holding the katana perpendicular to the floor, bring it across to the right side of your body and thrust the kissaki behind you. This is done with the hamon pointing upwards and the blade kept close to your right side. Now, pivoting the top part of your body, extend your arm behind you and thrust to the enemy's solar plexus. (See Figure #36.)

4. Bringing your right leg back so that both knees are on the floor, and with your back still facing the enemy, pivot on your left foot 180°. Step forward with your right leg again. You are now facing your enemy. Take hold of the mune with the palm of

Fig. 35

your left hand and push upward against the enemy's left wrist,
(See Figure #37; Figure #37A is a closer view of this action.)

5. Let the back side of the katana swing down beside your right
    leg and twist your right wrist, taking hold of the tsuka with
    your left hand over your head. Allow the tsuka to pivot in the
    palm of your right hand. Raising the katana high, almost to

Fig.   36

Fig.   37

Fig. 37A

arm's length, prepare for your downward stroke. Figure #38 shows completion of the downward cut.

6. Execute chiburi in the same manner as the previous katas.
7. Figure #39 Shows the start of kaishi and Figure #40 shows the finish.
8. Execute Taichi in the same manner as in the previous katas.

Fig. 38

Fig.　39

Fig.　40

Kata Number Eight
Ten Te
Heavens Hand

1. As you are walking, an enemy pulls your katana from the saya and tries to strike you with it. You immediatley extend your right hand. The palm is inward. Next, step out with your right foot. (See Figure #41.)
2. When the enemy starts to attack, take hold of the tsuka from the bottom side by placing your right hand between his hands. Next, pivot on the ball of the right foot and step behind the right leg with the left and turn 180° counter-clockwise. (See Figure #42.)
3. Constantly pressing forward with your right hand to prevent the enemy from regaining his balance, step across in front of his knees with your right foot, forcing him to press his stomach

Fig. 41

against your right hip. Keeping the cutting edge of the katana away from you, make a circle with your right hand and bring

Fig. 42

Fig. 43

the katana to your right hip. Simultaneously, lift your right leg, as in Judo's Harai-goshi. Before the enemy hits the floor, place your left hand on your saya. (See Figure #43.)

4. Now, pulling the tsuka from his hands, place the kissaki in the koikuchi, starting the return. (See Figures #44 and #45.)

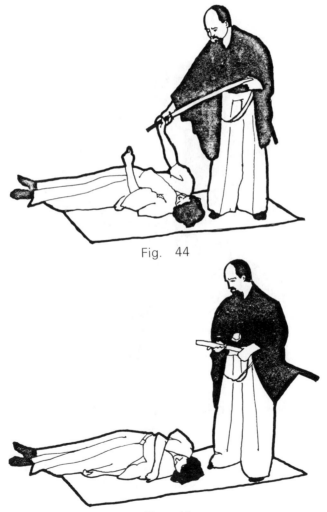

Fig. 44

Fig. 45

CHAPTER FOURTEEN

Kataoka Gengoemon Takafusa   (Ronin of AKO)

Kendo Kata

Kenjutsu Kata

I have included the Ipponme Kata, or the First Kata of the All-Japan Kendo Federation, in this book to show the reader the difference between Iaijutsu and Kenjutsu. Because there is some debate on the issue I cannot say with certainty whether or not the katas in kendo are Kenjutsu. But two of my Sensei agree that they are, so I must concur.

Figure #1-Ya the attacker and Tow the defender, kneeling opposite each other, katana on the right side with the cutting edge away from them.

Figure #2-Ya and Tow, bowing to each other, presenting their right hands to the floor first.

Fig. 1

Fig. 2

Fig. 3

Figure #3-Taking hold of their katana with the right hand, thumb on the tsuba and cutting edge up, then rise, using the right leg. Next, facing the flag or honored guest, bow from the waist.

Figure #4 without moving the sword position, each man turns his back on the other and takes nine steps, turns to face the other and bows. They now place the katana on their left sides, sliding it through their obi, cutting edges up, thumb still on the tsuba and feet together.

Figure #5 and #6 -Ya and Tow. Both start out at the same time using their right feet and take three steps forward. All this time they maintain eye contact. They now assume the Sonkyo position.

Fiure #6 shows the drawing of the swords. The first five to six inches of the tip of their blades must cross and the point of the blade point at one another's neck.

Figure #7-They rise to a standing position, keeping their chudan or center position and placing their left feet to the rear. They now lower the tips of their swords so that each man's sword is pointing

Fig. 4

Fig. 5

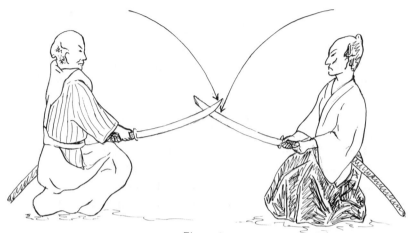

Fig. 6

Fig. 7

to the left knee of his partner. Holding this position and starting with the left foot, each man takes five steps to the rear, keeping eye contact at all times.

At this ten-step interval, each man brings his katana to the chudan (center) position. After holding this position for about a five count, they are now ready to start the kata.

Ya on the left brings his katana to the jodan position as well but does not move his feet. Tow's right foot is still leading. (See Figure #8.)

They now take three steps forward, Ya starting with his left and Tow with his right foot. This will bring them close enough to the chudan position that the tips or kensen would meet.

In this jodan position (Figure #8), Ya makes his attack by stepping forward with his right foot and delivering a head or shomen cut to Tow. He stops the cut about even with Tow's right

Fig. 8

Fig. 9

knee. (See Figure #9.) Tow, sensing Ya's attack and reacting at the moment, starts his movement. Tow steps back with his left (rear) foot one step, letting the right foot follow naturally. He simultaneously shifts his hands backwards slightly. This movement allows Ya's sword to pass in front of him and he evades the cut.

Ya now steps forward with his front right foot and delivers his own shomen cut. (See Figure #9.)

Figure #10-Ya lowers the tip of his sword so it is pointing to Tow's rear foot in the gedan position, while taking one step back with his left foot. Tow advances one step forward with his left foot, keeping the kensen of his katana to the center of the attacker's face.

Tow now takes one step to the rear with his left (front) foot and assumes the jodan position. (See Figure #11.) Note that Ya stays perfectly still while Tow is performing this move. He does, however, maintain eye contact.

Ya and Tow now assume chudan position. (See Figure #7.) Then both men lower the tips of their katana. (See Figure #12.)

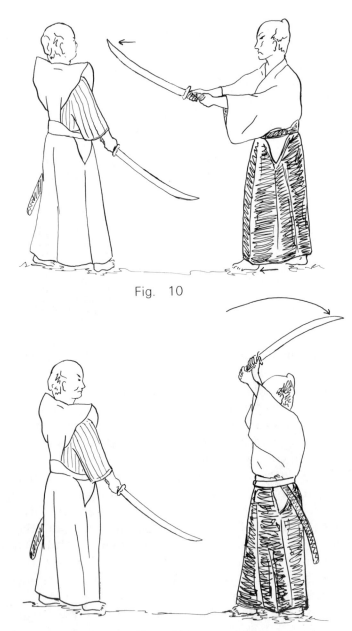

Fig. 10

Fig. 11

Beginning on the left foot, each man takes five steps to the rear. This concludes the Ipponme Kata.

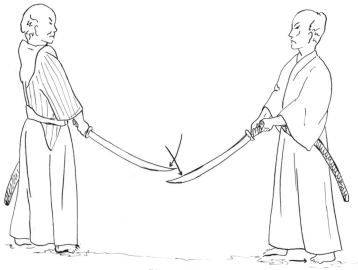

Fig. 12

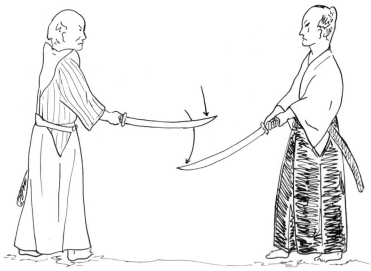

Fig. 13

CHAPTER FIFTEEN

Ohishi Kuranosuke Yoshitaka   (Ronin of AKO)

Chushingura
The Story of the Loyal Forty-Seven Ronin

"The Treasury of Loyal Retainers"

One of the most-often told and well-known Samurai stories in all Japan is "Chushingura" or in English "The Forty Seven Ronin." Now ronin literally means a "Wave Man" or "one who is tossed up on the endless sea." He has no master, therefore he comes and goes endlessly. In 1701, in the month of February, there lived a Samurai by the name of Asano Takumi-no Kami, who was the lord of Ako Castle. This was a time in Japanese history when the people enjoyed absolute peace and the country grew in wealth and prosperity. The militaristic spirit was nearly gone. The Shogun who ruled all of Japan had become more interested in luxury than in tradition and most of the Japanese people followed his example all, that is except the brave military Samurai. The spirit of bushido still lived in their hearts.

The Mikado having sent an Imperial ambassador to Tokyo, Asano Takumi-no Kami and another Samurai by the name of Kamei-Sama were ordered to receive and entertain him and his party. These two lords were not experienced in the proper procedure of entertaining such nobility, so they sought out a man by the name of Kozuke no-Suke who, they knew, was well versed in these matters. For many years he had taken part in these types of receptions. Now, Kozuke no-Suke was a man of greed and unbeknown to Asano, Kamei-Sama had bribed Kozuke to provide him with good advice. Asano was a Samurai of great honor and the notion of bribery never entered his mind. After not receiving any kind of payment from Asano, Kozuke grew angry and repeatedly made fun of Asano, causing him to make mistakes. One day when Asano was taking instructions, Kozuke proclaimed, "Asano, you are nothing but a village fool. Here, let me find something more suited to your wits. Tie the cord of my hat." To this Asano could hold his temper no longer and drew his short sword and attacked Kozuke, cutting him upon the head. Kozuke ran down the hall in

Asano Attacking Kozuke

fear of his life with Asano in pursuit. Catching Kozuke, Asano again struck out with his short sword, this time cutting the shoulder. Just as he was about to deliver the finishing blow, a Samurai by the name of Kajikawa Yosobie caught Asano from behind and wrestled him to the floor, allowing Kozuke to make good his escape. As soon as Kozuke was safe and his wounds attended, he ordered the arrest of Asano for the attempt on his life. According to the law, just the drawing of a sword in the shogunal court was a capital offense, so Asano was immediately given over to Tamura-Ukyo-dayu, lord of Shinoseki in Mutsu, a small suburb of Tokyo to wait the results of a deliberation of his offense. The decision came that very afternoon, an unusually swift verdict: Asano was ordered to commit seppuku immediately. He was taken to a small garden in the courtyard, where inspectors and seconds were appointed on the spot.

As Asano stepped upon the mat, (the place for the ceremony) he asked for paper and pen. This was brought to him without delay and he composed a poem which read:

Frailer far than the tender flowers
That are soon scattered by the wind,
Must I now bid a last farewell
And leave the general spring behind?

With this he laid down the writing material, lowered the top of his kimono, tucking the sleeves under his knees and put an end to himself.

Outside the gate of Kozuke Castle there waited a Samurai by the name of Kataoka-Gengoyemon whose job it was to accompany Asano, his Lord, to and from the castle each day. Upon hearing of his lord's sentence, he immediately ran back to his lord's quarters in the city and reported the news of Asano's death to Kayano Sempei and Hayami Tozayemon, two of Asano's retainers. They in turn made their way to Ako Castle, which in those days was a four and a half days' journey. When they arrived at Ako, Kayano reported immediately to Ohishi Kuranosuke, who was the head Samurai at the Castle.

"Ohishi!" Kayano shouted, "We have failed our lord Asano. He

Asano Composing Poem

was sentenced to seppuku four days ago for attacking lord Kozuke in the palace. Kill me, Ohishi, I beg you, I am not trustworthy."

Ohishi, lifting him by his kimono from his knees to his feet, shouted, "What do you mean, Asano is dead? Tell me again, you worthless peasant, tell me and stop your whining like a woman." As Kayano tried to explain with tears running down his cheeks, Ohishi hit him with all his might. "You were sent to protect our lord Asano and this is how you repay his kindness," said Ohishi, looking down on the floor where Kayano lay. "I should take your worthless life here and now." Ohishi reached for his sword. Kayano, remaining prostrate, jerked back his kimono so that his neck would be exposed to the blow of the oncoming katana. But to his surprise the blow did not fall. When he finally looked up he could see that Ohishi had been joined by Hara Sayemon and Oishi Sezayemon and they were trying to explain the exact circumstances which culminated in seppuku for their lord.

Ohishi slowly slid his katana back in his saya and told the two men to gather all the retainers in the Castle for a meeting in the Pine Corridor. Then Kayano saw Ohishi looking at him again, and he again extended his neck. But instead of the sword's edge, Kayano felt a warm hand on his shoulder. Turning his head upward Kayano saw a firm but smiling face looking down upon him. "Kayano, I know how you feel and I am truly sorry for the harsh words I spoke," Ohishi said, "But now I have an important mission for you." Lifting Kayano to his feet, he continued, "I want you to go to Teppozu Castle near the river Sumida and tell our lord's wife what has happened this day. Quickly reaching into his kimono, Ohishi gave Kayano some coins and bid him a speedy return. Then turning he started towards the Pine Corridor, knowing he must break the news to the awaiting Samurai.

When Kayano arrived at Teppoza Castle, it was only to find that his lord's wife had already received the news of her husband's death and had shaved her head that very day in preparation to become a nun under the name of Yozei-in. She would spend the rest of her years praying for her departed husband's soul. More important, Kayano thought to himself, was the news that Kira Kozuke no

Suke had sent word to his father-in-law at the Imperial Castle of what had happened. He was sure that Asano's retainers would take reprisal on him for the death of their lord, so he requested as many Samurai as could be spared to come to his aid. With these extra warriors he could withstand the oncoming attack.

With this most important infomation, Kayano remounted his horse and headed back to Ako Castle. Kayano kept thinking to himself as he raced through the still night, "I must not let my lord down again. If there is going to be a battle as Kozuke-no-Suke suspects, I must not be late. This time I will run under each sword of my lord's enemies and kill until I am killed." He could not help smiling to himself as he lashed out with his small whip. "Faster and faster, you brave and noble horse, take me faster. I must not be late this time."

When he arrived at Ako Castle, it was late afternoon of the fourth day. He saw no one and a chill grew into a cold sweat across his body. "No," he thought, "they have gone! How could they leave without me?" Just as he was dismounting, there came a most welcome sound to his ears: Ohishi Kuranosuke's voice. "Well Kayano, I see that you have returned to us. How did our lord's wife receive the news?" Kayano quickly related everything that had taken place, being sure not to omit any small details. "Well done, Kayano, yes, well done indeed," Ohishi replied.

To this Kayano replied, "What decision have you reached on the revenge of our lord?" Ohishi reached up and ran his hand over the top of his head. He stopped his hand over his mouth and mumbled something which Kayano could not make out.

"I beg your forgiveness, but I could not understand what you said, Ohishi."

"It is of no importance now, Kayano, of no importance—Let me tell you what has taken place in your absence. As you know I summoned all the retainers of the castle to a meeting and informed them of the whole affair. After this, we discussed how everyone should commit seppuku, but they could not agree and started arguing among themselves. So I have decided to hold the Castle to the last man against the government officers when they come to confiscate our lord's belongings. I have decided to divide our lord's war funds amoungst his Samurai. "To this Ohishi reached in his kimono and handed Kayano his share of remaining money.

But, instead of Kayano taking the money, he hit Ohishi's hand, scattering the coins about the garden path. Ohishi jumped back, startled, "What is the meaning of this? Do you not wish to die here in honor, defending your lord's castle against the oncoming government officials?"

"Die! Die!, you speak to me of dying, when I was ready to die by your own hand just a few days ago for letting our lord and clan down? But now you talk of dying here and letting our lord's killer go free. No, I am not afraid of dying, but let it be with a purpose. Let me die under the sword of my lord's enemy, not here by some government agent whom I have no quarrel with."

Ohishi reached out his hand and took Kayano by the arm, "My loyal friend, please let me explain. I am afraid I have not been completely truthful with you." There was a slight pause.

"What you do not know," Ohishi continued, "is that after I passed out the war funds, many of the so-called Samurai of our lord ran away and there are only sixty of us left. Now that I know your true feelings, there are sixty-one, am I not right, Kayano?" Kayano could not help showing his delight. He smiled broadly. He leaped in the air and then quickly turned to Ohishi and said, "When do we strike? Tonight? Tomorrow? When, Ohishi? Tell me quickly."

"Not so fast, my good friend," Ohishi replied. "Let us go into the courtyard where the rest are waiting and I will reveal to you my plan."

As all the retainers gathered in the court yard, Ohishi Kuranosuke began to unfold his well kept secret of how they would revenge their lord and kill Kira Kozuke-no-Suke. They each swore oaths of secrecy and pledged their lives to the fulfillment of their assigned tasks. They all agreed to surrender the castle and then disperse to become "ronin."

Now Kira Kozuke-no-Suke was so sure that he would be attacked by Ako Castle Samurai that he took every precaution and sent spies to watch the retainers' every move. But when they reported back to Kozuke-no-Suke that all the retainers had left the castle and had taken to the countryside to become ronin, he flew into a rage. "What do you mean," he stormed, "ronin! Do they think I am so stupid that I cannot see into this foolish plan? Now go and find and watch them listen to everything that they say, and do not come back here until you find out their plans. Now get out of my sight until you have some information." At this he threw down his cup of tea and left the room.

As he entered the adjoining room, he summoned Dōkyo Shojū, one of his most trusted retainers. When he saw Dōkyo enter the room he quickly motioned him to come to his side. Sake was prepared for them. Looking around to make sure they were alone, Kozuke-no-Suke began to pour sake and, speaking in a soft voice so that no one could hear, he said, "Dōkyo, I am sure that Asano's head Samurai, Ohishi Kuranosuke, will be the guiding light behind the attack against me, so it is most important that you find him and keep me posted on his every move. We cannot be too careful until this whole matter is settled." Taking hold of Dōkyo's arm and looking into his eyes, he asked, "Do you understand, my good friend, just how important this mission is?" "Yes, my lord," Dōkyo replied. "I will leave this very evening, and do not worry if Ohishi-san is planning an attack of any kind. I will discover it, and we will be ready. With this they lifted their sake cups and Dōkyo departed.

For his own safety-because he expected treachery—Ohishi knew that he had to leave Ako as soon as possible for if anything happened to him, his plan would never bear fruit. He packed his things, took his wife and children, and headed for Yamashina, a village east of Kyoto, the old capital of Japan.

Arriving in Yamashina he purchased a house and land to make everyone think he had intentions of staying permanently. One day while he was working in his bonsai garden, he received word that Fuwa Kazuemon had married the daughter of the architect of Kira Kozuke-no-Suke's house and that the ronins now had the complete plans of every room in their enemy's dwelling. At this Ohishi was delighted, but there was disturbing news in that Kozuke-no-Suke was still protected by his father-in-law's Samurai and had sent Dōkyo Shojū, his most trusted retainer, to spy on him.

Ohishi sat down on a rock in his garden and began to ponder. "So this old fox is still watching and listening to my every move. Good, it could not be better. For what Kozuke-no-Suke did not know was that many of the ronin had separated from their families and had gone in to the world as tradesmen or artisans and had also distinguished themselves in the occupations so that it was easier for them to gain entry to his mansion. They, of course, were spying. Ohishi knew, too, that several of his retainers had left the league one by one until there were only forty-seven men left to carry out his plan. But this would be enough to do what had to be done. The most important thing now was to keep Kozuke-no-Suke completely off-guard.

Ohishi, determined to throw the enemy completely off his trail of revenge, started living a life of apparent despair. It became a common thing to see Ohishi in the brothels of Kyoto or Osaka, drunken and disorderly. One evening after he returned from one of these outings, Ohishi's wife pleaded with him:

"Ohishi, my beloved husband, please! You must stop this drunkeness; it is ruining our lives and there is little money left to live on. I can understand your plan, but you have gone too far. We cannot live like this!"

"We?" Ohishi shouted, "We cannot live like this? Well, we do not have to! Get out! Get out and stay out; take the children too! I do not want to see any of you here again!"

"You cannot mean this! Ohishi-san," his wife begged, "Please do not send us away. I am sorry for having said these things. Please let us stay"

But Ohishi's mind was made up, though his heart was broken, for he loved his wife and children. It had to be done, he thought. It would be much better for everyone; the family would be safer away from here. After his family had left Yamashiro, Ohishi brought a woman by the name of Okanu to his house to become his mistress. Okanu was known throughout Kyoto for her beauty and pleasing manners and knew nothing of Ohishi's plot of revenge. One night when Ohishi was returning home drunk, he stumbled and fell flat on his back in the street. While he was trying to rise on one knee, a Samurai who knew Ohishi happened by. He stopped and, looking down upon him, proclaimed in a loud voice so that others stopped and started to laugh, "Is this the great Samurai Ohishi Kuranosuke, head retainer of my beloved friend, lord Asano Takumi-no-Kami? No! This cannot be him, for the Ohishi-san I knew would be too busy revenging his lord's death, instead of lying about in the street drunk."

To this Ohishi said nothing, but reached out his hand for help. Instead, the Samurai lifted his foot, and placing it on Ohishi's left shoulder, gave him a hardy push. Ohishi fell backwards. "This is indeed where you belong," the Samurai proclaimed, and spit upon him.

When Dōkyo Shojū heard of the incident, he reported back to Kozuke-no-Suke immediately. They were convinced that the Ako clan would do nothing, that there was not a true Samurai amongst them. No Samurai of any class would have permitted someone to spit upon him without killing the offender on the spot, even if it took the last ounce of life in his body. So with this news Kozuke-no-Suke felt more secure and returned half of the borrowed guards to his father-in-law. He did, however, feel that it would be wise for his spies to keep their ears and eyes open as a precaution. Eventually, however, they grew weary of watching and became less interested in the Ronin's movements.

When Ohishi heard what his enemy had done and that Dōkyo had stayed in Edo with his lord, he knew that the time was at hand. Now that he was not watched so closely, he slipped out and went to Osaka. There he had a meeting with his old friend Amanoya Rihei, a merchant. He supplied Ohishi with all the weapons that would be needed to carry out his plan of revenge. After returning home Ohishi sent word for all forty-six men to meet just outside of Edo at a place they had previously agreed upon.

It was January 19, 1702 when the last man, Kayano, came through the small door to where the rest were waiting. Ohishi could not help but feel delight when he saw his old friend bowing to him.

He motioned for Kayano to join the rest. Ohishi began to speak. "My fellow retainers, we have long awaited this moment. There is no need to speak of the hardships we have all endured, but that is all in the past. Now we must look to the plan of revenging our lord." As Ohishi looked around the room he motioned to Naka-miya Kansuke, "Did you bring the plans of Kozuke-no-Suke's home?" Nakamiya handed them to Ohishi. He had made two sets so that everyone could study them closely. They laid out the plans on the floor, and everyone gathered around eagerly.

Ohishi resumed, "Very well, my loyal friends. Chiba here has informed me that our enemy is going to give a tea party tomorrow night, so we know that he will be home. Tomorrow night after the party, when everyone is asleep, we will strike. If you were not able to bring your weapons, take one of these and make yourself ready."

As Ohishi handed out the weapons, he proclaimed "Do not forget to write your documents,[1] explaining who we are and what we are going to do. We do not want to be mistaken for bandits."

He then divided the group into two parties to study the house plans. "This is my plan. As you can see by the drawings, we must be very careful not to let anyone escape through the rear.

They might bring reinforcements from Kozuke-no-Suke's father-in-law. We do not want any more blood shed than is necessary. About half an hour before the attack, I want you, Hara-san and Fuwa-san, to go tell all of Kozuke-no-Suke' neighbors what we are planning to do; this will keep them from worrying about being attacked too. I really do not think we have anything to worry about from them as my reports indicate that they all dislike him as much as we do. We will divide ourselves into three groups. I will take one and my son will take another. The third will be made up of eight men. These eight men will be stationed on the walls." Ohishi pointed at the map, "Here, here, here and there. The other four will be stationed here and here so they can see anyone who might try and escape using the front or back gates. It will be their duty to make sure that no one escapes. These eight will be our best archers. My group will come in through the front gate here. The other group will enter through this fourth back gate on the west side there. The signal will be the beating of the drum in the Yamaya Soko manner. We probably will not receive much resistance until we get to this point, the courtyard to the main house. But no matter, we must push through until the two groups join together here. If any one should find Kozuke-no-Suke before I, blow your whistle. Do not kill him until we can be sure it is he and we can all be there to witness the act. Are there any questions?" Ohishi slowly looked around the room but no one spoke. He smiled, and getting up from the box on which he was sitting, opened it. "Good," he said, "then let us all have a last drink together." He picked up two sake bottles.

Early the following morning, at two o'clock, all the retainers began to gather and by two thirty everything was ready for their long-awaited attack. Snow was falling heavily by the time the small band reached Kozuke-no-Suke's mansion. Ohishi motioned for everyone to gather around him and speaking in a low tone, he addressed Hara. "We will give you thirty minutes, no longer, to awaken the neighbors and inform them, as we have discussed. Everyone else to their stations. Remember if the household should be awakened before I have sounded the attack, proceed as planned. With this bright clear moon, we should have no problems. Kill only when necessary; dispatch only those who offer resistance." He pulled his katana from its resting place and waved it high in the air. "We must not fail!" he vowed, and the small band began to disperse through the heavy snow.

The minutes seemed like hours as the ronin awaited the signal, and though it was bitterly cold, no one seemed to feel it. All at once the attack sound broke the silence of the night, and inspired the retainers with inexplicable courage. Kayano was the first man to reach the guard house at the gate. With swords in hands, he slid the door quietly open with a foot. The men pushed past him. He then quickly stepped inside. Taking his short sword and lightly poking it at the blanket laying on the floor and with his long sword raised above his head in a ready position, he spoke, "Give us the keys to the gate and no harm will come to you." The man, half asleep, rose on one elbow, "What is going on here?" Give us the keys to the gate," Kayano replied, this time pushing at the man a little harder with his sword. "I do not have them," answered the man in a shaky voice. The other ronin were standing with their swords pointed at the other two guards and watching every move. "We have no time to argue with you," Kayano said, "We are here to revenge our lord, Takumi-no-Kami." Before he could continue, the guard reached for his katana resting in its rack. But he was far too slow, and his severed arm fell to the floor. His loud cry of pain was silenced by Kayano's second cut across the neck. Kayano turned to the other two guards. "Well, what about you? I suppose that you know nothing about the keys either" he surmised, while shaking the blood from his sword. "Never mind, tie them up. We will break the gate down." Returning the short sword to its saya, he turned and left the room.

In the few short minutes that passed, Kayano could hear the cries of battle on the other side of the wall. "Hurry up in there," he commanded. "We do not want to be the last to arrive at the main house." Once past the gate, Kayano group broke up into several smaller groups. The fighting was spreading throughout the compound. As Kayano turned a corner, he found himself facing two of Kozuke-no-Suke's Samurai. Quickly pulling his short sword, he charged straight forward. The surprising suddenness of his charge allowed him to cut one of the Samurai in half. But, as he turned to face the other, he slipped in a pool of blood, landing on his back. Immediately the Samurai attacked with an overhead swing of his blade. Kayano could see the sword coming down threatening to deprive him of his sworn revenge. Taking hold of the upper torso of the dead Samurai lying beside him, he pulled it atop himself as a shield. The blade struck, and though he feared the blade might cut through the impromptu shield, the body held. As the Samurai prepared for his second attack, Kayano grabbed a handful of blood and sand, and flung it into his attacker's face. Rolling to his side, he made a low horizontal cut dividing the attacker from his front foot. Jumping to his feet, he finished the Samurai off with a second cut and ran to the courtyard of the main house.

When Kayano arrived in the courtyard, he discovered small duels of two and three men everywhere. One battle caught his eye.

244

Dokyo-Shoju Holding off the Ronin with ease

On the porch of the main house, Kozuke-no-Suke's head retainer, DōKyo Shojū, had three of the ronin fighting for their lives. He was astounded. Dōkyo was fighting like a mad man, but using his swords with such ease, parring and countering each attack as though it were child's play. The ronin were slowly being driven back off the porch. This enraged Kayano. He commanded at the top of his voice, "Stop this retreating at once! You made a vow to give up your life to revenge our lord's death and yet you back away from death as if there were a choice." The words cut through the falling snow like an icy wind and taking hold of the ronins, pushed them Forward. It was not long before they had pushed Dōkyo back up the steps. He was now fighting for the inches of ground on which he stood. Finally, Kayano picked up a lance, and threw it between the ronin, hitting Dōkyo in the neck. As they watched, Dōkyo dropped his short sword, grabbing hold of the lance, trying desperately to yank it from his neck. He swung wildly with the katana in his other hand. For a moment, Kayano feared Dokyo might yet kill the ronin with his fierce persistance in living. Then as when a light breeze causes the cherry blossoms to fall from the tree, Dokyo fell forward, down the steps, dead at the ronin's feet.

Kayano, thought to himself, how brave a Samurai they had slain! But his thoughts were quickly broken off by Ohishi's voice, "Over here Kayano, quickly! Kayano ran quickly to Ohishi's side where most of the other ronin had already gathered. Ohishi raised his sword in the air. "We have won," he shouted, "but what good is this victory if Kozuke-no-Suke has escaped. He cannot be found anywhere," Ohishi said, circling his sword to encompass the estate. "Spread out and search again. If he is not found, we will meet here and commit seppuku. Now go, and let not this battle have been fought in vain!" Looking at Kayano, Ohishi pointed at the main gate, "We will look again in there." They reached Kozuke-no-Suke' sleeping quarters but without a clue to their enemy's whereabouts. Suddenly Kayano shouted excitedly "It is warm! I tell you it is warm! Here, feel this blanket, I tell you it is still warm." Ohishi gave a signal and the ronins came running from every direction to the sleeping quarters.

"Kozuke-so-Suke is not far from this very spot," Ohishi shouted. "Look everywhere, tear up the floors and ceilings if necessary, but find him!" There was new hope for the ronin now, and they tore the room apart in their search. Moments later Muramatsu Kihei shouted to the others, "Look here, behind this silk screen on the wall. There is a hole big enough for a man to crawl through!" Muramatsu took his sword and ran it deep into the cavity, but to no avail. He then crept inside the small tunnel probing ahead with his sword. After sliding along on his hands and knees for about ten feet, he came to an opening that led into a small court yard. Still there was no sign of Kozuke-no-Suke. The other ronin started pouring out of the tunnel into the courtyard. Muramatsu spotted a small woodshed in the far corner and approached it, shouting "Kozuke-no-Suke, come out! I, Muramatsu Kihei Hidenao, ronin of Ako, know of your cowardice in fleeing, but now you have been found. I demand that you come out and meet your responsibilities!"

There was no response from inside the small shed. Before Muramatsu could say another word, Kayano pushed him to one side, kicked in the door and began to stab savagely into the darkness with his katana. There came a loud cry of pain and Kayano emerged with blood dripping from his sword onto the white snow. "Drag him out where we can see him for the coward that he is!" Kayano exclaimed. Two ronin complied, dragging an elderly man dressed in white sleeping dress from the darkness of the shed. As Kayano raised his sword to put an end to the old man's life, Ohishi shouted, "Stop, you have half killed him already ," pointing to a large cut on the old man's side. "We are not animals," Ohishi continued. Taking the old man by the arm, he led him to the center of the small courtyard and asked Muramatsu to fetch a lantern so they might make sure that this was truly Kozuke-no-Suke.

As the small band of brave ronin gathered about, Muramatsu returned with a small but adequate light. Holding it in front of their prisoner, Ohishi grasped the old man's top-knot and held his face to the light in the falling snow. "Can anyone identify this man as

Kozuke-no-Suke, killer of our lord, Asano Takumino-Kami?"

Silence followed and a gust of wind blew the snow in frigid eddies about the courtyard. Then Kayano shoved aside several of the ronin. "I know this man to be Kozuke-no-Suke. I say let us waste no more time! Cut off his head and let us be on our way." "All in good time, Kayano," said Ohishi, reaching into his kimono. He withdrew a small tanto and handed it to the old man.

"We were the retainers of our departed lord, Asano Takumi-no-Kami, who came to you last year for instruction. Because of the evil in your heart, he was forced to die by his own hand. We now demand that you commit seppuku with this same tanto which our lord himself used in his own ceremony.

The old man dropped the knife in the snow and leaning away from it, began to beg for his life. Ohishi tried desperately to persuade him to kill himself with honor, but to no avail. Seeing that the man was hysterical and that any further persuasion was useless, Ohishi picked up the small knife and motioned to Kayano and Muramatsu to hold the old man's arms and head down. Kozuke-no-Suke began to scream and beg for his life at the top of his voice, but none of the ronin listened to his pleas. Ohishi, removing the saya from the small knife, proclaimed for everyone to hear, "I take the head of our sworn enemy—Kozuke-no-Suke—in the name of our beloved lord Asano-Takumi-no-Kami."

In a moment the cries for mercy were silenced. The head was then wrapped in a cloth and placed in a bucket. The small band marched out of the courtyard carrying the bucket. The snow had stopped. No words were exchanged between the ronin as they filed out but when Kayano reached the small gate he could not help but look back at the headless body, thrashing about as a fish out of water, thinking to himself that justice had finally been served. "Now at last I will be able to meet my lord eye to eye," he thought.

It was now nearly six o'clock in the morning. The attack had lasted about two hours and to the surprise of Ohishi, they had not lost a single man. As the band of ronin marched in pride carrying their trophy in the bucket, the word of the attack spread like fire. Soon people began to cheer them along the roadside as they passed.

The Ronin's Washing Kozuke Head

They arrived at the temple of Sengakuji, their lord's burial place south of Yedo, by mid-morning. After they reported their deeds and intentions to the head priest, they carefully washed the bloody head in a well outside of the temple grounds and then proceeded to their lord's grave. Ohishi gathered everyone about the grave and reported in a loud voice, as though their master were still alive, all the circumstances of the revenge.

When the ceremony was concluded, the small band gave themselves up to government officials.. The date for the execution of their sentence was January 24, 1702. (The courts divided the small band into three groups: seventeen were turned over to Hosokawa Etchu-no-Kami, lord of Chofu, and twenty were turned over to Okino-Kami, lord of Matsuyama) The rest were sent to Mizuno Kenmatsu, lord of Okazaki. The total number of ronin taken in charge by the daimyo was forty-seven. On the tenth of March, 1703, they were ordered to commit seppuku in succession in the mansions of the respective daimyo who had them in charge. They were buried at Sengakuji temple beside the tomb of their beloved lord, whom they had served so well.

You may ask, after counting the tomb stones, "There are forty eight stones. Who is the other one?" Here we have a true Samurai also—one who carried the code of Bushido to the end along with the ronin. His name was Bukkō Takuan. He came to the grave site one summer morning and standing before Ohishi Kuranoshuke's grave, proclaimed, "I, Bukkō Takuan, who knew not of the plot of revenge you carried in your heart last year and who kicked and spit upon you causing you more disgrace than I can bear, do hereby beg your forgiveness." After which he took a small dirk from his obi and stabbed himself until he was dead. The priest of the temple, knowing of his grief and wishing to comfort his spirit, buried him beside the ronin.

Even today people still flock to visit the graves and pray for these valiant men. The Japanese people will never forget the memory of these faithful and valiant clansmen. Once every sixty years the priests hold a two-month festival commemorating these heroes' deeds.

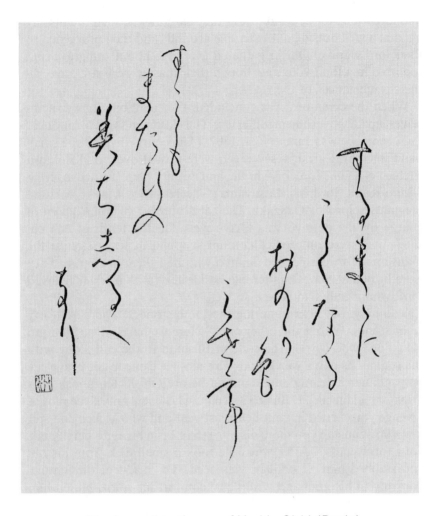

The farewell testimony of Yoshio Oishi (Ronin).

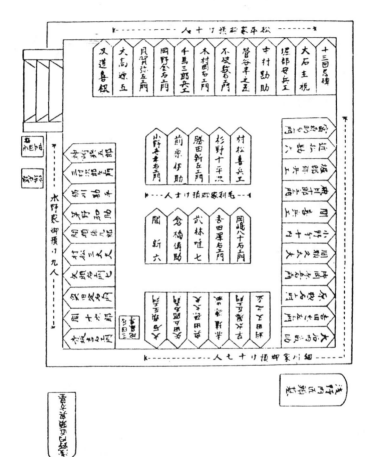

The graves as they are in the temple.

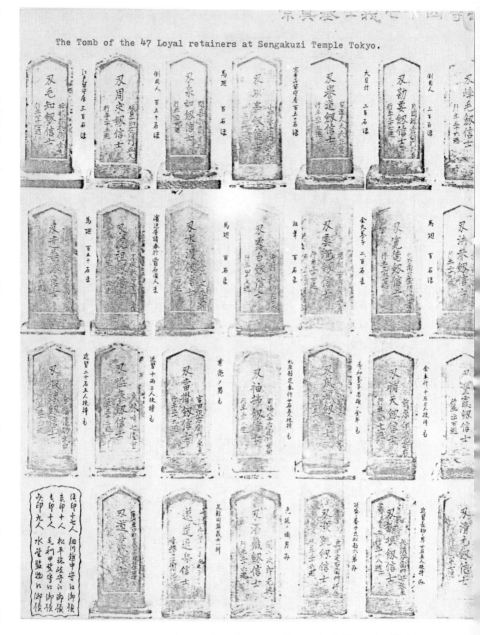

The Tomb of the 47 Loyal Retainers at Sengakuji Temple, Tokyo.

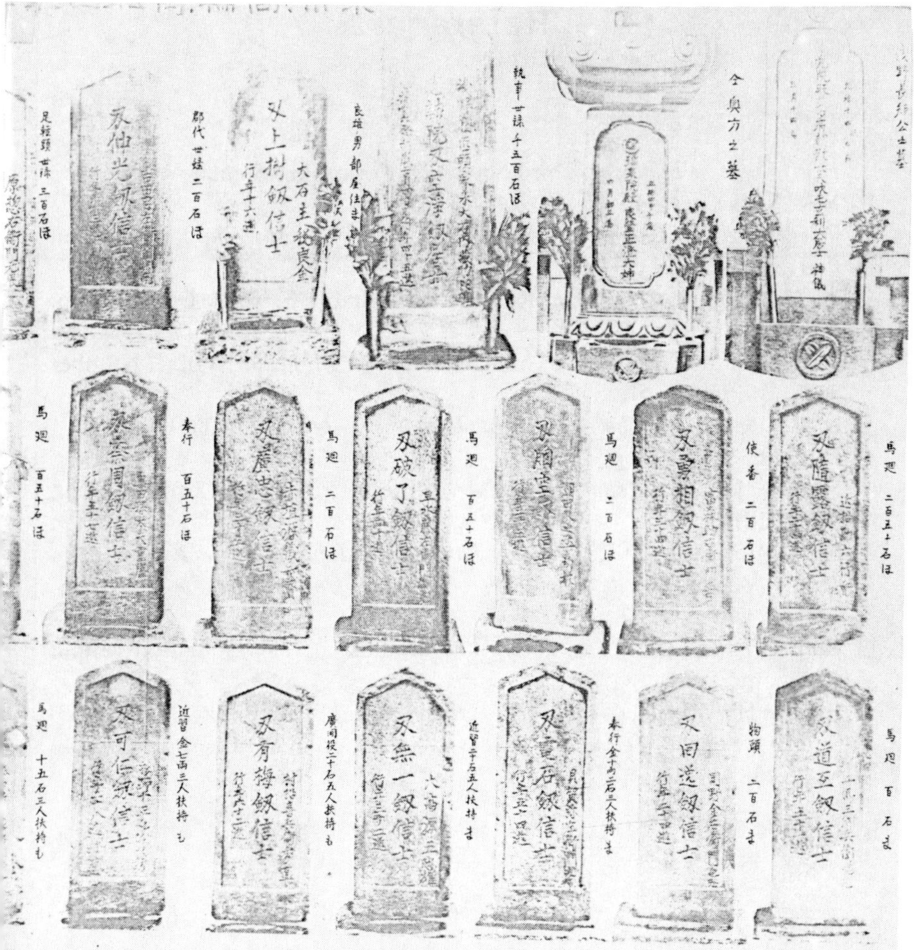

仝 奥方之墓
執事 世禄 千五百石ほ
良雄男 部屋住ま
郡代 世禄 二百石ほ
足軽頭 世禄 三百石ほ
馬廻 二百五十石ほ
使番 二百石ほ
馬廻 二百石ほ
馬廻 百五十石ほ
馬廻 二百石ほ
奉行 百五十石ほ
馬廻 百五十石ほ
物頭 二百石ま
奉行 金十両三人扶持ま
近習 二十石五人扶持ま
廣間役 二十石五人扶持も
近習 金七両三人扶持も
馬廻 十五石三人扶持も
光延ノ次男 も
徒士 五両三人扶持み
奉行 五両三人扶持 み
徒士目付 五両三人扶持 み
正明ノ男 み
秀直ノ男 み

References

Essays in Zen Buddism, Third Series, D. T. Suzuki, (Samuel Weiser Inc., New York), p. 144.

D. T. Suzuki, *Zen and Japanese* Culture, (Princeton, N. J,: Princeton University Press, 1971).

W. D. Jennings, *The Ronin* (Rutland, Vt.: Charles E. Tuttle Co., 1968), p. 129.

Rodger Fitlock, "Japanese Cross," *Black Belt Magazine,* Vol. 7, Number 5, (May 1969), p. 49.

B. W. Robinson, *The Arts of the Japanese Sword,* C. E. Tuttle co. Inc., Rutland, Vt., 1971, p. 15.

Donn F. Draeger, *Asian Fighting Arts* (Berkley Publishing Corp.: N. Y. N. Y.) p. 101.

A. B. Mifford (Lord Redesdale), *Tales of Old Japan, Charles E. Tuttle Co. Inc., Appendix A – Account of the Hara-Kiri from a rare Japanese MS, Third Printing, 1970.*

Van de Wetering J., The Empty Mirror, Boston, The Houghton Mifflin Company, 1974.

Eugene Herrigel, *Zen in the Art of Archery,* (Bantheon Books, N. Y.: 1953.

Shunryu Suzuki, *Zen mind, Beginner's Mind,* John Weatherhill Inc., 149 Madison Ave., N. Y., N. Y., 1974. p. 21.

Glossary

AIKUCHI: dagger without tsuba.
ASHI: foot.
BUJUTSU: working parts of Iai-do.
BUSHI: old term for Samurai.
CHIBURI: removing blood from sword.
CHING: limits.
CHUDAN: Center readiness with sword.
DAISHŌ: two matched swords.
DATTO: removing the katana from obi.
DIRK: Small knife used in seppuku.
DO: way.
DOJO: school or training hall.
EDO: old name for Tokyo.
EMBU: Practice of Martial Arts.
HA: cutting edge of sword.
HAKAMA: Samurai divided skirt.
HANSHI: Iai Master.
HAPPO-GIRI: style of eight cutting directions.
HAPPO-NO-KAMAE: style of eight directions.
HARAI-GOSHI: hip throw.
HARA-KIRI: everyday word used for abdomen cutting.
HASSO: ready position with the sword tsuba even with your chin.
HENOBE: formal Samurai dress.
HEYAZASHI: small dagger.
HOJO JINSUKE: said to be the founder of Iai in 1600.
IAI: drawing.
IAI-GOSHI: letting the waist sink.
IAI-HIZA: sitting with raised knee.
JODAN: overhead position with sword.
JUTSU: art-method or technique.
KAISHAKU: second in seppuku.
KAMI-NO-ASHI: upper foot nearest the shrine.

KAMIZA: place of honor in dojo.

KATA: form of practice.

KATANA: long sword.

KENDO: sword way.

KENSEI: sword saint.

KESAGIRI: scapular cut with sword.

KIRITSUKE: cutting.

KISSAKI: tip of sword.

KIZU: flaws on sword.

KODOGU: hardware on sword.

KARASUGUCHI: crow beak crack at top of swood.

KOJIRI: cap on the end of saya.

KOSHI-ITA: stiffener in back of hakama.

KYOSHI: one rank below Hanshi.

MEIJI: late nineteenth and early twentieth century in Japan.

MAI: inscription on tang.

MEN: head.

MENUI: ornament in sword handle.

MIYAMOTO: Musashi Samurai (1584–1645).

MORI-RYU: a style of Iai-do.

MOROTE-SUKI: two-handed-thrust.

MU-GAI-RYU: style of Iai-Jitsu.

MUNE: back side of sword eight inches from the tip.

MUNEN: to have no thought.

MURAMASA: sword maker.

MUSHIN: to have an empty mind.

Myōyō: spiritual attainment.

NOTO: returning sword to saya.

NUKIKATA: drawing the sword.

NUKITSUKE: the draw

OBI: belt.

REI: formal bow.

RONIN: masterless knight or Samurai.

RYU: style.

SAGEO: cord on saya.

SAINEIKAN: Imperial Palace Dojo.

SAMURAI: knight or soldier of Japan.

SANPOGIRI: three-way cut.

SAYA: scabbard.

SAYABIKI: pulling the saya to meet the sword guard.

SEIZA: sitting in place.

SENSEI: teacher.

SHINOGI: back side of sword.

SHINZA: shinto altar.

SHINZEN: a Shinto term (before a god).

SHOGUN: war lord.

SONKYO: sitting on balls of feet.

SEPPUKU: formal word used for abdomen cutting.

TACHI: slung sword.

TAIJO: procedure of leaving the practice area.

TAITO SHISEI: standing with sword in belt.

TANDEN: abdomen center of power.

TANG: end of handle under sword.

TANTO: dagger.

TE: hand.

TEITO SHISEI: formal standing.

TOMOE: circle.

TOREI: formal bow to the sword.

TOW: defender in kata.

TSUBA: sword guard.

TSUKA: handle of the sword.

TSUKA-ATE: striking with end of sword handle.

TSUKAGASHIRA: end of sword handle.

TSUKAHARA BOKUDEN: swordsman (1490–1572).

UCHIKO: limestone for cleaning swords.

UKENAGASHI: warding off an attack.

USHIRO: behind.

WAKIZASHI: short sword.

WAZA: technique.

YA: attacker in kata.

YAKIBA: temper line on sword.

YOKO: side.

ZEN: A Buddhist sect.

ZANSHIN: spiritual preparation.